The Life of St. Maximilian Kolbe

Apostle of Mass Communications

William LaMay

Scripture quotations in this book are from the New Revised Standard Version copyright 1989, Division of Christian Education of the National Council of Churches of Christ in the United States of America.

Edited by Mary Kathleen Glavich, SND
Cover designed by Peter Tonon, Jr.

Photo Credits: Marytown Press, Libertyville, IL (pp. 105-110; 112-121; 123-126).

Illustration on pages 128-152 used with permission of Nerbini International, Lugano, Italy.

Death Certificate reprinted with permission of The State Museum Auschwitz-Birkenau in Oswiecim.

ISBN-13: 9781794305663

Printed in the United States of America

Contents

Dedication

This book is dedicated to all those who paid the ultimate price in the concentration camps of World War II, to all those who survived these camps but continued to suffer the physical and emotional effects of their imprisonment, and to all those in the armed forces who were injured or killed in their efforts to free those imprisoned in these camps. May they be eternally blessed and never forgotten.

No one in the world can change Truth. What we can do and should do is to seek truth and to serve it when we have found it. The real conflict is an inner conflict. Beyond armies of occupation and the hecatombs of extermination camps, there are two irreconcilable enemies in the depth of each soul: good and evil, sin and love. And what use are the victories on the battlefields if we ourselves are defeated in our innermost personal selves.

~ Father Maximilian Kolbe, O.F.M., Conventual

Introduction

No one has greater love than this, to lay down one's life for one's friends.

~John 15:13

On October 10, 1982, a picture-perfect, warm day in Vatican City, the sun shone on more than two hundred thousand pilgrims from all over the world gathered in Saint Peter's Square. A large tapestry of Blessed Maximilian Maria Kolbe was displayed on the façade of St. Peter's Basilica.

While high-ranking Vatican officials, other dignitaries, and devotees of Kolbe were in attendance, one person stood out. He was seated in a wheelchair in the front row as a special invited guest of Pope John Paul II. Franciscek Gajowniczek, an eighty-one-year-old Catholic survivor of Auschwitz, was there because on July 30, 1941, Father Maximilian Kolbe offered up his life in exchange for his.

The crowd was awaiting the appearance of the Polish pope for the canonization Mass of his fellow countryman, when Blessed Maximilian Maria Kolbe would be declared Saint Maximilian Maria Kolbe. The pope was born in 1920, two years after Kolbe was ordained a Franciscan priest. Many wondered whether Blessed Maximilian would be considered a martyr. Finally, the pope emerged wearing red vestments, indicating a martyred saint.

The main theme of Pope John Paul II's homily during the Mass was Father Kolbe's heroic act of love in which he resembled Jesus, who died for all people. From his youth, Father Kolbe was filled with a great love of Christ and desired martyrdom. The pope mentioned that Father Kolbe's devotion to the Immaculate Conception led him to found Marian movements in Poland and Japan. The Holy Father concluded by stating that Father Kolbe's death was a sign of victory and a witness of the Church in the modern world. Therefore, although Father Kolbe was previously venerated as a confessor, he would now be venerated as a martyr.

This book, *The Life of St. Maximilian Kolbe, Apostle of Mass Communications,* recounts the life of Saint Maximilian Kolbe. In it you will learn how his personal experience of an apparition of the Virgin Mary sent him on the path to a religious vocation with the Franciscan order and to the mission of spreading Marian devotion that eventually reached to all four corners of the globe. Father Kolbe was dedicated to saving souls through Christ and his mother by making both physical and spiritual sacrifices. As a seminary teacher, he told his students that his ultimate goal was to become a great saint through his love of fellowman. He attained this goal when, as a prisoner in Auschwitz, he died in a starvation bunker so that another prisoner, a stranger to him, could live.

In all likelihood, Kolbe's academic brilliance would have gained him a Nobel Prize had he decided to use his God-given gifts to pursue a career in mathematics or science. Instead, this humble priest was inspired by the mother of Jesus to embark on the path of sacrificial love and use his knowledge of philosophy and theology to convert souls to Christ through Mary. His chosen path took him through years of pain and suffering, culminating in living out Christ's words: "No one has greater love than this, to lay down one's life for one's friends" (John 15:13). Given the prestigious life of academics, few would ever take this courageous path. But this Polish saint born of humble beginnings did so, thereby attaining sainthood and earning the title Martyr of Charity. Saint Maximilian Kolbe now serves as an icon of Christian life and love.

How This Book Came About

As a lifelong Catholic and a licensed amateur radio operator, call sign K3RMW, a question suddenly occurred to me: Is there a patron saint of ham radio? Not really expecting to find there was, I sat at my computer and did an Internet search. To my great surprise and delight, I discovered that a Polish saint, a Franciscan priest by the name of Maximilian Maria Kolbe, was the official patron saint of amateur radio. Father Kolbe, who was martyred at Auschwitz in August of 1941, held an amateur radio license issued by the Polish government in 1938 with call letters SP3RN.

After this exciting discovery, I had to learn more about St. Maximilian Kolbe. I dove headfirst into the world of research, looking for every book and website I could find about him and his amateur radio station. The more I found, the deeper I dug, and soon was thoroughly engrossed in the story of this brilliant but humble priest and his unusual martyrdom.

Before I knew it, I had a growing desire to let others in the world of amateur radio know that a canonized saint was a licensed member of our hobby. I never considered writing a book before because I didn't think writing was one of my God-given talents. However, now the thought of writing a biography of St. Maximilian never left me, as though the Holy Spirit were giving me an assignment. Once I decided to proceed with this project, I began to build a library of books and an abundant collection of articles from the Internet and elsewhere about the saint's life and writings.

Over the course of several years, I disciplined myself to work on the book each day, even just for an hour or so. Now the book is finished, thanks to the help of those who put the icing on the cake. It all began with a simple question. I hope *The Life of St. Maximilian Kolbe, Apostle of Mass Communications* will introduce many people to St. Maximilian Kolbe, especially amateur radio operators, who, I think, will be as pleased as I was to know we have our very own patron saint.

Chapter 1

Birth of a Saint

Poland's strategic location in central Europe led to numerous invasions over the centuries. Troops constantly crossed the country to attack enemies on the other sides. In the 1890s, Poland had been partitioned by its neighbors Russia, Austria, and Prussia. The people's yearning to become an independent country gave rise to strong resistance movements. Poland's patroness, Our Lady of Czestochowa, called the Black Madonna, had seen them safely through many wars, and they turned to her again.

Although Poland as a sovereign nation did not appear on most nineteenth-century maps, the people were unified by their Catholic faith, culture, language, and patriotism. Despite its many battles, Poland welcomed those who were unwelcome in other European countries. For centuries it had the largest Jewish community in the world, one reason being that Catholicism was rooted in Judaism.

One of Poland's staunchest defenders and patriots was Julius Kolbe, who lived in the part of the country occupied by Russia. He was an ethnic German born on May 29, 1871, the oldest of four children. On October 5, 1891, Julius married Marianna Dombroska, a pious Polish girl born in 1870, whose father was a weaver. The wedding took place at Assumption Catholic Church in Zduńska Wola, Poland, a town about ninety-eight miles northwest of Krakow with approximately 15,700 residents.

Julius was outgoing and charitable with a great work ethic and a passion for music, especially the violin. He and his wife, known as Maria, were both active members of the Third Order of Franciscans founded by St. Francis of Assisi for lay members and now called Secular Franciscan Order.

Maria had no formal education because her family was too poor to afford the cost of schooling. Instead she was schooled at home while performing household duties. She became a self-employed midwife and a successful community nurse, using natural remedies to cure illnesses, thanks to permission from the local physician.

From childhood, Maria desired to be a nun. However, to suppress Polish patriotism, the Russian czar promoted only Russian Orthodox churches. He closed all Catholic convents, and so Maria decided to marry.

After the Kolbes were married, they rented a second-floor flat of a two-story, wood cottage. They used one room for their looms, which they operated from early morning to early evening six days a week. The remaining rooms were a bedroom and a kitchen.

A year after the Kolbes' marriage, their first son was born. Not surprisingly, they chose to name him Francis after the founder of the Franciscans. The next child, also a boy, was born on January 8, 1894, and named Raymond. Maria insisted that he be baptized that same day because she feared he would die without benefit of the sacrament. In that era, the infant mortality rate was high. Many diseases were incurable, and for some others, many doctors and hospitals did not have access to the treatments.

After contacting the pastor, the Kolbes wrapped Raymond in warm clothing and a blanket to protect him from the bitter cold and walked to the Church of the Assumption of the Blessed Virgin Mary a few minutes away. At 4:00 PM the baby was baptized by Father Kapalczynski at the baptismal font in the narthex of the same church where the Kolbes were married twenty-six months before. Little did they know that their newly baptized son would die a martyr forty-seven years later on the eve of the Feast of the Assumption of the Blessed Mother.

The year following Raymond's birth, Julius decided to move to Lodz. Due to declining economic conditions in their local community, the family business was beginning to falter, while there were improvements in industrialization in Lodz. There Julius figured he would have more secure employment in one of the textile factories. So the Kolbes gathered up all of their belongings and headed for their new home in hopes of a better future for their growing family.

On January 29, 1895, shortly after the move to Lodz, a third son was born to Julius and Maria, and they named him Joseph after the saintly foster father of Jesus. Unfortunately, conditions in Lodz proved to be less than desirable. For one thing, the Kolbes lived in an overcrowded tenement house, subjecting them to threats of diseases such as rickets and tuberculosis, which were more common in industrial cities. Also, the many factory furnaces sent unhealthy smoke and other pollutants into the air. To make matters worse, their children were exposed to various crimes and the onset of materialism, which potentially could corrupt their faith and values. All things considered, the Kolbes made the conscientious decision to move away from the trappings of the big city to the small village of Jutrzkowidice situated near Pabianice, a suburb of Lodz.

Now Julius was able to move into a small home on property large enough to cultivate crops for their own use and to sell. There Maria continued to work as a midwife and nurse. She often didn't charge for her services in order to be faithful to the vow of poverty the Kolbes took when they became lay Franciscans.

Julius and Maria also opened a small variety store in a building on their property, which was close to a road leading to the Krusche-Ender textile factory and convenient for those on their way to and from work. In addition, the Kolbes marketed their homemade textile goods to the cloth market, providing additional financial support.

When manufacturing improved substantially in Pabianice, the Kolbes were forced out of the textile market. Fortunately, Julius was able to find a full-time job as a weaver with the Krusche-Ender textile factory.

The fourth son, Walenty, was born in the family home on November 1, 1897. Tragically Waltenty died the following year on

November 20, leaving the Kolbe family in shock and grief. Maria explained death to her three young sons by telling them that God calls little children to heaven, but we don't always understand why. She reminded them that Walenty was baptized. Now God wanted him with him and in God's time, they all would be reunited.

Walenty's body was placed in a small wooden coffin, which was set on a catafalque at the altar of St. Matthew Church in Pabianice. Family and friends gathered, weeping, and the priest began the Requiem Mass, offering Walenty's soul to Christ and asking that he be with the angels and saints. The priest prayed for peace and consolation for all those present that heartbreaking day as they struggled to understand the death of someone so young. After the Mass, the mourners processed to the nearby cemetery in the dreariness and cold of that winter day to say their last goodbyes and place Walenty's body in its final resting place.

On May 19, 1900, Maria, now thirty years old, gave birth to the Kolbes' fifth and final child. After much thought and discussion, they decided to name him Antoni after St. Anthony of Padua, a Franciscan priest—an appropriate choice given their membership in the Franciscan Third Order. St. Anthony was born in Lisbon, Portugal, on August 15, 1195, the feast of the Assumption of the Blessed Mother. An outstanding preacher and theology teacher, he passionately defended the Catholic faith and brought about numerous conversions before dying on June 13, 1231, at the age of thirty-six.

Following Antoni's baptism, family and friends gathered in the Kolbe home, where Maria read a passage from the Bible that reflected the life of St. Anthony:

> We brought nothing into the world, so that we can take nothing out of it; but if we have food and clothing, we will be content with these. But those who want to be rich fall into temptation and are trapped by many senseless and harmful desires that plunge people into ruin and destruction. For the love of money is a root of all kinds of

> evil, and in their eagerness to be rich some have wandered away from the faith and pierced themselves with many pains.
>
> *~1 Timothy 6:7–10*

Then Maria read St. Anthony's comment on these verses:

> A voluntary poverty instills stamina, but the wealth erodes our spiritual strength because humans, rather than being masters of their wealth, soon become the servants of what they possess. For example, if one suffers loss of material and possessions and is grieved by that loss, he is a slave to his grief as he formerly has been a slave to his material possessions.

Now with four children to feed, clothe, and educate, Julius and Maria decided to take a vow of perpetual abstinence and devote the rest of their lives to serving God through prayer, work, and study while guiding their children through their faith journey. They placed three of their children in the fifty-member boys' choir at St. Matthew Church. The virtuous Maria cultivated devotion to the Mother of God in her children. Every day they prayed the Angelus, the Litany of Loreto, and the Rosary.

For the next few years, the Kolbes' lives were settling down. Then another tragedy struck the family. Antoni became ill and died on July 27, 1904, at age four, two days after Francis celebrated his twelfth birthday. In their grief and pain, the family questioned why God would allow this to happen when they were so devout. The funeral was a repeat of Walenty's. This time the pastor Fr. Szulc offered the Mass and led the procession from the church past the Krusche-Ender textile plant onto New Cemetery St. (now Kilinski St.) to the cemetery where Walenty had been buried almost six years before. In sharp contrast to the cold weather during Walenty's burial, a sunny sky and a warm summer breeze accompanied Antoni’s, perhaps giving his parents and brothers hope for resurrection and eventually reunion with the two boys.

Chapter 2

The Apparition and Calling

Like all of the Kolbe children, Raymond was taught from an early age to be respectful and giving. He was, however, rambunctious, a trait that challenged his mother's somewhat limited patience. Although usually obedient, Raymond sometimes was mischievous and prone to childish pranks. Strange as it might seem, Raymond's track to sainthood began with one such caper that involved an egg.

St. Francis of Assisi loved God's creatures and had a special affinity with them. Raymond loved and admired this saint, and so he too had a great fondness for animals and nature. Because St. Francis talked to birds and even gave them a sermon, Raymond desired a bird of his own, not one in a cage, but a free-roaming one. His creative mind led him to take an egg from his kitchen cupboard, go to the henhouse of his neighbor, Mrs. Zalewski, and place the egg under one of her hens. He figured that the hen would hatch the egg and he would have a chick. He carried out his plan without his mother's knowledge or the neighbor's permission to enter her henhouse.

Unbeknownst to Raymond, Mrs. Zelewski happened to observe him periodically making trips to her henhouse. Puzzled by these trips, she visited Raymond's mother to solve the mystery. Of course, Maria confronted Raymond about the visits, and he explained his actions. Sternly Maria said, "You will not take another egg from the cupboard. You'll not go into Mrs. Zalewski's garden or chicken house. Do you understand, Raymond?" "Yes, Mother," the boy replied as tears welled up in his eyes.

Raymond received a sound spanking, the normal punishment for breaking any of the Kolbe household rules. He also suffered the pain of disappointing his mother, whom he loved greatly. This pain was likely intensified when she said to him, "Raymond, what will become of you?" Little did Maria know how her words of frustration would impact her son's future, not to mention countless people throughout the world. Her words and obvious distress brought about a radical change in Raymond's behavior.

A short time later, Raymond walked to church and knelt in prayer before a statue of the Blessed Mother. Tearful and remorseful, he implored his spiritual mother to help, saying, "O holy Mother, I am a bad boy. I caused my mother to cry. Whatever will become of me?" Suddenly, to his surprise and wonderment, the Blessed Mother appeared before him in radiant beauty, her face full of tenderness and compassion. She held a crown in each hand, one white and the other red. The white crown stood for purity, and the red crown represented martyrdom. Mary asked Raymond to choose one. After some thought, he answered with the zeal of a future saint, "I choose both." Pleased, the Blessed Mother smiled and then disappeared.

Apparitions of Mary, both public and private, have occurred throughout the world. Among the more famous are her appearances in Guadalupe, Mexico, in 1531; Lourdes, France, in 1858; and Fatima, Portugal, in 1917. Before approving any apparition, the Catholic Church authenticates the reports through extensive investigations. An apparition, even an approved one, is not a dogma; a person is free to believe it or not.

Ever since Raymond's spiritual encounter with the Blessed Mother, his personality was different. His mother noticed that he was quieter, more obedient, and more prayerful. She saw him weeping while he was kneeling before the picture of the Blessed Mother at their home shrine. What has happened to my child, she wondered. Because the family had dealt with the loss of two boys, she was worried that Raymond was ill and did not want her to know.

Finally, Maria questioned Raymond about his changed behavior. Reluctantly he confessed that her words "I do not know what will become of you" had a profound effect on him. He also revealed that he had seen an apparition of the Blessed Mother offering him two crowns when he visited the church.

Overwhelmed by her son's account, Maria reflected on what had happened and how it affected Raymond. She concluded that his experience was genuine. Raymond had spoken often about his desire to become a priest. Now Maria would support him in this quest. For Raymond, the only question that remained was when and under what circumstances he would become a martyr.

Chapter 3

Journey to the Priesthood

Because of the Kolbes' limited finances, Francis, the oldest son, was the only one to attend school, a local commercial school. His parents hoped that he would someday become a priest. The other sons were educated by Maria at home, where they also helped run the family variety store and delicatessen. The local parish priest, Father Vladimir Jakowski, instructed them in Latin and the Catholic catechism. He recognized Raymond's high intelligence. Because Raymond wanted to be an altar boy, he worked hard at mastering Latin, which was required for that role. Although Raymond did not have regular schooling, his diligence in focusing on academics would garner a reward that came about in a surprising way.

Once while Maria Kolbe as a midwife was caring for a mother, she needed a poultice, a medicated mass applied to relieve pain. Maria summoned Raymond and sent him to the local pharmacist, Mr. Kotoski, with the formula for the medication. Raymond gave the pharmacist the formula in Latin. Duly impressed, later that day Mr. Kotoski visited the Kolbe family and told them how amazed he was at Raymond's grasp of Latin. He inquired if it would be possible for Raymond to attend a regular school. On learning that the Kolbe's overstretched budget did not allow for this, Mr. Kotoski said that he considered Raymond an exceptionally bright young man and offered to tutor him in science and mathematics at no cost. Julius, Maria, and, of course, Raymond were delighted with this news and gladly accepted the offer. The extra instruction would certainly pave the way to Raymond's goal of becoming a priest.

Raymond began his lessons with Mr. Kotowski immediately. Besides deepening his knowledge of math and science, Raymond also learned German, knowing that this new language would prove beneficial in later years. After this private schooling, Raymond was able to go to a technical school for a short time.

When Raymond was about thirteen years old, he and Francis went to a mission retreat at St. Matthew given by Conventual Franciscan Father Peregrin Haczela. At the end of the mission, Father Haczela announced that his order was opening a high school seminary in Lwow in the southeast part of Poland. The Franciscans were looking for young men willing to devote their lives to serving God and the Madonna. Because both Francis and Raymond were interested in religious life, this was exhilarating news. It seemed like a plan made in heaven, given that their parents belonged to the Third Order of Franciscans.

Francis and Raymond eagerly talked with the priest about going to the high school. All the pieces seemed to be falling in place. The two boys had been planning to attend the seminary and having a sound educational background, they were qualified for the junior seminary. Besides, they had a great love for Our Lady of Czechtochowa, and the Franciscans were involved in the Marian movement. But the boys needed their parents' approval and blessing.

Soon after the mission, Francis and Raymond told Julius and Maria about the opening of the seminary high school and how going there seemed to be a golden opportunity to pursue their dreams of a religious vocation. The parents considered this idea and no doubt realized that this was the answer to their own prayer. That tuition and all related expenses were free was another persuasive factor. With no barriers in place, Julius and Maria finally gave their consent for Francis and Raymond to attend the seminary.

The two boys were elated, but their excitement was somewhat dampened by the fact that they would be leaving their loving parents and other brother, not knowing when they would see them again. Nevertheless, they felt in their heart that taking this step was their calling and what the Blessed Mother wanted from them.

Julius decided to accompany his sons on the train through their occupied country because these were dangerous times in Poland and the boys had never traveled so far. Before long, Francis, Raymond, and Julius were boarding the train. Maria, with tears running down her face, embraced them and handed each one a bag of food and drink for the journey.

As the train pulled away, Julius, Francis, and Raymond waved white handkerchiefs. The young boys' emotions wavered between sadness and excitement. No longer would they have the comfort of their parents each day but would rely on their spiritual mother for security. Now as they traveled, they prayed to the Blessed Mother and her Son that they would reach the seminary safely.

Julius was fortunate in possessing a passport and could travel legally, but neither of his sons had one. They faced a perilous journey though potentially hostile territory, depending on prayer and faith in God and his Mother. The first leg of the trip was from Lodz to Krakow, about one hundred-seventy miles. After passing through Russian controlled territory, the train stopped. The group now faced the challenge of crossing the Austrian controlled border without the boys' passports.

With the help of divine providence, Julius came upon a farmer on a hay wagon who was traveling in the same direction. Julius explained that his sons were headed to the Franciscan monastery in Lwow without passports and risked being detected by security. The farmer graciously agreed to hide the boys beneath the hay. Prayers were answered! Francis and Raymond quickly climbed aboard the wagon and buried themselves under the pile of hay. Although the two boys were a bit uncomfortable, they and Julius arrived safe and sound in Krakow. There they stayed at a Franciscan monastery overnight.

As the sun began to rise over Krakow the following morning, Julius and the boys ate breakfast. Then they were driven to the train station accompanied by one of the Franciscan brothers for safety. The boys would travel the two-hundred-mile leg of the journey without their father. At the station, they hugged Julius good-bye, tears welling in their eyes, and then boarded the train. They waved to their father as the train pulled away, headed toward the minor seminary in Lwow.

Chapter 4

The Seminary

At the seminary Raymond relished the joy and the challenges of both the academic and spiritual life he encountered each day. His probing mind convinced his professors that he was an exceptional student. Among the forty students at the minor seminary, Raymond was known to be extremely bright, cheerful, and humble and was admired by his schoolmates. He adjusted well to life in the seminary. German was spoken at the school, so his study of this language proved beneficial. On one occasion, though, because of his German name, during a quarrel another student taunted, "You, German!" and Raymond burst into tears.

Raymond excelled in mathematics and the physical sciences and had a creative mind, especially when it came to science and space. Soon after Raymond's arrival, his companions would observe him in the seminary garden with a sketchbook, drawing pictures of spacecraft and how they could be propelled beyond earth's orbit. When asked how such heavy machinery could fly, Raymond explained that the force of the propulsion of the rocket could provide enough energy to boost the weight of the rocket. He used the example of a bird's body being lifted by its wings against the law of gravity. Finally, he won the skeptics over by pointing out the Wright brothers' success in 1903 and 1904.

One of Raymond's closest friends was his roommate, Bronislaus Strycznys, who was a year or two older than he. Later, Father Bronislaus recalled the following:

> My friend distinguished himself in school by his efforts and hard work. We students and especially our teachers marveled at his deep and usual grasp of mathematics. In no time he used to solve the most difficult mathematical assignments, ones that the rest of us and even the teachers need much time and paper to conclude. He was

> more than kind to us and ready to help us with our mathematical difficulties. No wonder he won our good will.
>
> Already, he anticipated the possibility of reaching the moon with a rocket and he thought of many other unusual inventions. (Patricia Treece, *A Man for Others: Maximilian Kolbe, Saint of Auschwitz, In the Words of Those Who Knew Him.* [San Francisco: Harper and Row, 1982], p. 8)

Father Bronislaus became a prisoner in the concentration camp at Dachau, Germany. Eventually he was transferred to the United States and died in Santa Maria, California, on August 14, 1974, thirty-three years to the day that Father Maximilian Kolbe died.

While engrossed in academic life, impressing his professors with his astuteness and unquenchable thirst for knowledge, Raymond had an underlying longing to become involved in seeking freedom for Poland. Julius Kolbe had instilled a strong sense of patriotism in his boys, teaching them Polish history. Raymond hoped that one day Poland would be a free and independent county, and he saw himself as an important part of bringing about that vision. An outstanding chess player, he viewed this talent as part of his training for the battlefield in case he chose a military career. At that time, however, there was no formal Polish army. Nevertheless, during his studies at Lwow, Raymond displayed his talents as a strategist. Through much time, thought, and effort, he once designed and built a cardboard model of a fortress that he proposed could be built around the city of Lwow to make it invulnerable to invading armies.

As a sixteen-year-old, Raymond was faced with a dilemma. He was forced to decide the kind of soldier he would be: a soldier for his country or a soldier for Mary Immaculate, his spiritual mother. Making that decision was no easy task because he loved both Poland and Mary. The time for deciding was drawing near.

With his gift of persuasion, Raymond convinced Francis that they should join the military. They agreed to inform the Franciscan Prior of their decision and headed to his office. Raymond continued seesawing about their choice and paced back in forth in front of the office a short time. Then the two brothers entered the office and sat in the waiting room. But divine providence intervened again. Suddenly the front doorbell rang, and a friar entered the room. He announced to the boys that their mother had just arrived and wished to speak to them in the parlor. Smiling broadly, Raymond and Francis hurried joyfully to the parlor and greeted their mother with hugs.

Maria announced the good news that their brother Joseph was going to follow in their footsteps and become a member of the Franciscan order. But that was not the end of the news. Enthusiastically she revealed that she and their father would also be serving God as a member of a religious community. She would move to Lwow and live with the Benedictine Sisters to be near her sons, and their father would attend the house of the Franciscans in Krakow. After three years with the Benedictines, Maria moved to Krakow and became a lay member of the Felician Sisters until she died in 1946.

At their mother's news, Francis and Raymond realized they would stay the course for religious life. After all, how could they disappoint their parents who had been praying and working that their sons would become priests? Their hopes for a military life to fight for Polish independence might just be on hold, and God might still find a way to integrate it into their future somehow. Only time would tell.

After an emotional good-bye to Maria, the brothers ran to the Prior and asked to be invested with the Franciscan habit. Instead of becoming knights for their native Poland, they would become knights for Mary. Raymond accepted the fact that his future led to his ultimate goal, total service to God as a religious and, hopefully, a martyr.

On September 11, 1910, Francis and Raymond received Franciscan habits from Father Peregrine Haczela and became novices. Raymond appropriately was given the name Maximilian (also spelled Maksymilian) after a young third-century saint in North Africa who was martyred for refusing to enlist in the Roman army because he was a soldier of Christ. Kolbe later added Maria to his name. During that school year, Max, as he was called, wrestled with scruples, a form of spiritual nervous breakdown. Always sensitive to faults and sins, he saw himself as very imperfect and became highly self-critical. This obsession was cured when he was told to reveal any anxiety to his roommate, Bronislaus, and to follow his advice.

The next year when Max was seventeen years old, he made first vows, promising poverty, chastity, and obedience. After finishing his secondary schooling, he was sent to study in Krakow. The teachers there recognized his intellectual gifts, and in 1912, he was handpicked to study in Rome with six other seminarians. Maximilian was honored, but initially declined because he had symptoms of tuberculosis, a common and often fatal disease then. He believed that Rome's climate would have an adverse effect on his health. Nevertheless, after some prayer and reflection, he acknowledged that studying in Rome was God's will mediated through his superiors, and he had taken a vow of obedience. He reasoned that God's will takes precedence over one's own will. He went to Rome, a decision he no doubt never regretted.

Chapter 5

Rome and the Militia Immaculatae

At first Maximilian attended the prestigious, Jesuit-run Pontifical Gregorian University. While he suppressed his dream of fighting for Poland, two of his family members took action. In 1914, his father left the Franciscan monastery and became an officer in Jozef Pilsudski's Polish Legions fighting the Russian army for Poland's independence. Julius was captured as a traitor by Russian soldiers and presumably hanged that same year at age forty-three. Francis took a leave of absence from the seminary and joined the Polish Liberations Army as an intelligence officer. During the war he was wounded and, instead of returning to religious life, married and had one child. In 1943, he died a prisoner in a German concentration camp.

On November 1, 1914, All Saints' Day, Maximilian made his final vows. In 1915, he graduated summa cum laude with a doctorate in philosophy. He was twenty-one years old, although because of his youthful face, he could have been seventeen. Maximilian then enrolled in the Franciscan International College, where he majored in theology with the goal of becoming a theologian.

During his seven years studying in Rome, Maximilian was known for his genius. It was said that he would have become a great inventor had he not chosen the religious life. One of his math teachers, Grushala, remarked, "It was a pity that he was going to become a priest since he had so many great talents." Another teacher sadly said, "Now all he will have to do is to count columns." Maximilian's blueprint of a space vehicle capable of flying to the moon or photographing space impressed one of his professors. Confident that a spacecraft could become a reality, this teacher suggested that Maximilian apply for a patent for his idea. Teachers and students alike believed that if Maximilian had chosen a career in science, he would have fulfilled his dream. Some of them lived long enough to see him become a canonized saint instead of a great scientist. It could be said that Maximilian reached the heavens, but not by means of a spacecraft.

Maximilian was somewhat naïve, but he was intuitive in social matters. He often expressed concern about the industrial revolution, communism, growing materialism, and mass media. Nevertheless, Maximilian took a positive approach and considered how some of these could be used to benefit people. Indeed, he took advantage of them later in promoting Catholicism and devotion to the Blessed Mother.

Maximilian's spiritual life was also deepening. Others noticed his humility, simplicity, and devotion to the Eucharist and to Mary. When he went to chapel to pray, he sat in the front pew so as not to be distracted during his meditation. He was troubled by the Franciscan Order's need for renewal. As time passed, Maximilian grew in love for God and strove to be obedient like the Mother of God. While studying in Rome, Maximilian rose to the next level on his path to the priesthood by being ordained sub-deacon in 1916.

Going back to his early childhood, Maximilian had a special devotion to the Mother of God, as evidenced by his childhood apparition of her. On January 20, 1917, while praying in the seminary chapel, Maximilian felt the call to establish a Marian organization that would perpetuate the work and desires of the Virgin Mother. Coincidentally, this was the seventy-fifth anniversary of the Blessed Mother's appearance to Alphonse Rattibone, a French Jew who converted to Catholicism and became a Jesuit priest and missionary.

On October 16, 1917, four days after Mary appeared to three children at Fatima, Portugal, Maximilian gathered together six other friars who wished to dedicate their lives to Mary and formed an International Marian movement. He named the group Militia Immaculatae or Knights of Immaculate, sometimes called M.I. This name honored the Immaculate Conception. On December 8, 1854, the Church had declared the doctrine of the

Immaculate Conception: from the time Mary was conceived, she was free from all sin— original sin and personal sin. Maximilian began the custom of referring to Mary as the Immaculate.

The purposes of the M.I. were to convert sinners, heretics, schematics, especially Masons, and to promote holiness under the sponsorship of the Blessed Virgin Mary Immaculate. When Pope John Paul II canonized Father Maximilian, he said that membership in the Militia means the complete dedication to the Kingdom of God through Mary Immaculate. The members wore the Miraculous Medal, which the Blessed Virgin had revealed to St. Catherine Labouré during an apparition in Paris in 1830. The medal is inscribed with the prayer "O Mary, conceived without sin, pray for us who have recourse to you."

Maximilian had written the program for the M.I. on a small piece of paper. The seven friars signed it, professing their allegiance to the M.I., and dedicated themselves to work towards recruiting other friars to this movement.

On Sunday, April 28, 1918, Friar Maximilian, together with several other Franciscan friars, lay prostrate on the floor of the church of St. Andrew of the Valley in Rome and were ordained as priests by Cardinal Basil Pomili, the Papal Vicar for the Archdiocese of Rome. The next day, Father Kolbe said his first Mass at the altar of the church of Sant' Adrea della Fratte, the same church where Alphonse Ratisbonne witnessed the apparition of the Blessed Mother. The year 1918 also saw the end of World War I and the establishment of Poland as a sovereign state. A year later saw the beginning of the great influenza that spread world-wide killing hundreds of thousands including thousands of U.S. soldiers returning home from World War I.

The work of the M.I. progressed very slowly. Two of the first recruits died of the flu. Father Kolbe, too, had to deal with health issues. While in Rome, Father Kolbe had been coughing up blood often. He was diagnosed with tuberculosis and required a period of hospitalization. During his time of recuperation, he rewrote programs for the M.I. and submitted them to the Father

General of the Franciscans, Most Reverend Dominic Tavani, for approval. Once approved, the proposal was sent to Rome for the pope's review and approval. Finally, on March 28, 1919, Pope Benedict XV officially blessed the Militia Immaculatae. On April 4, 1919, Father Travani gave it his official approval and strongly suggested that the M.I. be shared especially to the youth. Approvals complete, Maximilian began the mission of promoting the Blessed Mother and ultimately holiness of life.

In July 1919, Father Kolbe was awarded a doctorate in theology and was ready to head home.

Chapter 6

Teaching and Chaplaincy

Father Kolbe boarded a train back to Krakow to embark on his mission of serving God by bringing others to Christ through the Blessed Mother. On the journey he prayed and wondered what was in store for him at the monastery. He hoped to fulfill his lifelong dream of becoming a missionary, but his vow of obedience required him to accept whatever his heavenly Father had planned for him.

Once Father Maximilian arrived, he reported to the superior and was given the assignment of teaching at the seminary, applying the knowledge he had gained over his years in Rome. Despite his disappointment, he accepted God's will and in the depths of his heart remained hopeful and optimistic that someday in the near future his wish to be a missionary would be granted.

The war in Poland had led to a shortage of coal, the primary heating source. The seminary buildings where Father Kolbe taught were damp and cool. Consequently, this aggravated the tuberculosis in his lungs and kept him from projecting his voice well. Students complained that they could not hear his lectures. He moved slowly and was nicknamed Marmalade and Molasses. His ill health was a growing concern to Father Kolbe and to his superiors, who feared he would die from the menacing disease.

Unfortunately, at that time no drugs were available to control the symptoms or cure the disease. The only remedy was bedrest in a sanatorium located in a dry, cool location. Thus, Father Kolbe's superior sent him to Zakopane, a mountain resort several hours south of Krakow and away from the pollution of the coal-fired factories and other industries in that big city.

Restraining a patient like Father Maximilian, who was so driven to save souls, became a daily challenge to the medical staff at Zakopane. Prior to his leaving for the sanatorium there, his superiors instructed him not to conduct any work related to the

M.I. Although Father Kolbe obediently complied with that order, his zeal compelled him to use his training and knowledge to bring hope and comfort to the ill people around him. He became chaplain not only at his hospital but at others in the town. He was adamant about not sitting idly by when so many souls were suffering and he could provide compassionate care and also try to convert them.

One sanatorium Father Kolbe visited was designated primarily for college students. Most of them were lapsed Catholics or atheists, victims of the growth of communism in neighboring Russia. Father Kolbe recognized that this was a prime opportunity for conversions. He used a different and more restrained approach to convert the students. As he went about his visitation, he provided the students with books and engaged them in informal conversations, allowing them to express their opinions about their faith or lack of it. His low-key efforts and charming manner resulted in the conversion of many of those he befriended. Unfortunately, the director of one sanatorium was an avowed atheist and prohibited priests from being on the property. Undaunted, Father Kolbe conned his way in by telling the doorman that he needed a certain book that was only available in the library there. Eventually, Father Maximilian was so successful that he gained the friendship of director, who then often invited him to come anytime.

A nurse at that sanatorium, Anna Wojtaniowa Gabas, took advantage of this priest who had gained access to the patients. She would call on him to offer the last rites to those who were seriously ill or expected to die. She recalled the following:

> Very sick, and hospitalized elsewhere himself, he was a true Samaritan. When I called him, he always came right away. . . . Many times this was in the depths of the night or during snowstorms, and he himself might have a fever. In the case of the dying, I noted he frequently came running without taking the time to dress adequately against the cold. I remember one night there was a violent

> rainstorm when I telephoned that there was no time to lose; he came with communion for a dying girl, not at all concerned about the rain or the mud and left happy.
>
> When he came to lead discussions . . . he conducted these in such a spontaneous and pleasant way that all of the sick, even those who had long ago abandoned any religion, loved him.

Father Kolbe gained many converts and baptized many others, including a young Jewish medical student on his deathbed. The man's mother, who had come to claim his body, was shocked and upset that she could not bury her son in the Jewish cemetery. Another patient, a nun, remarked about Kolbe, "When he said Mass for us, he gave the impression of being in direct touch with God. Just watching him at the altar made you aware of his sanctity."

On April 28, 1921, Father Kolbe left Zakopane and went to convalesce in the north central city of Nieszawa until November of that year.

Chapter 7

Publishing *The Knight*

Feeling well and refreshed that November, Father Kolbe happily returned to the seminary in Krakow to continue his mission. He embarked on a project to improve communications among the Catholic population of Poland and the surrounding countries. His plan was to publish a newspaper to counteract the Church's enemies and promote the M.I. Perhaps later he would take advantage of the emerging media, radio and movies. It would be the friars' responsibility to collect information for his newspaper and print it. For the friars, this was a bit radical. They challenged: "What about your vow of poverty? Where do you plan to get the money? Do you expect it will float down from heaven? Anyway, we have no press to print such a paper."

Although Father Kolbe managed to obtain his superior's approval for his proposal, he was not given the money to fund his project. The superior told him he would have to find a way to raise the funds but did offer to support the friars involved in the project with his prayers.

Wasting no time, Father Kolbe went begging from house to house and business to business, explaining to all who would listen about the importance of his mission and how it would honor the Blessed Mother. By the end of the week, miraculously he had raised enough money to print the first edition of the newspaper, which he called *Knight of the Immaculata* or simply *The Knight.* He and other friars, including his brother Joseph, now Father Alphonse, wrote the sixteen pages. Kolbe delivered the newspaper to a local printer, who agreed to print it. Unfortunately, the original cost of printing the newspaper had risen considerably due to sudden inflation in Germany and Russia. The war debts and reparations required by the Versailles Treaty had peripheral effects on Poland. The first issue bore the note, "As capital is lacking, we cannot guarantee readers that *The Knight* will appear regularly."

Father Kolbe's venture incurred a 500-mark debt and no money to pay for it.

When faced with challenges, Father Kolbe always turned in prayer to the Blessed Mother for help. His excitement over the production of newspaper was tempered by his superior's revelation of the large debt. Kolbe immediately walked to the basilica and knelt before the statue of the Virgin Mary. He prayed: "O Holy Mother, do not permit the Militia Immaculatae and our efforts to strengthen the faith to become an embarrassment to our Franciscan Order. We have worked diligently to achieve our goal. Do not permit economic circumstances beyond our control to frustrate this work which we have dedicated to thee."

As Father Kolbe got up, preparing to leave the church, he glanced over and noticed an envelope on the Marian altar. Picking it up, he saw these words written on the front: "For you, O Immaculate Mother." Upon opening the envelope, he found enclosed 500 marks. Thrilled, he ran to his superior and showed him the envelope with the money. The superior agreed that the money was the answer to his prayers and told Kolbe to give it to the printer.

In the fall of 1922, the Father Provincial assigned Father Kolbe to a friary in Grodno, a desolate area in northeast Poland, in hopes of helping the priest's continuing battle with tuberculosis. The site also afforded more space for printing. Two Franciscans were sent to help Kolbe. In addition to the work of publication, Father Kolbe was assigned parish work while the other two friars served in the monastery.

To meet rising costs, printers were changed five times that first year. Father Kolbe suggested that the friars could publish the newspaper less expensively if they had their own printing press. He knew he couldn't always depend on little miracles to pay a printer. At the same time, he was well aware that the Franciscans did not have the money to purchase a printing press. "Where would the money come from?" asked his superior.

Divine providence started the fundraising process through a visiting friar, Father Laurence Cyman, from the United States. Unlike other friars who were unimpressed by Father Kolbe's proposition and even mocked him for it, Father Cyman was interested in disseminating the Gospel of Jesus Christ through new Marian publications. As a result of an informal discussion with Father Kolbe while they walked through one of the friary gardens, Father Cyman offered to send $100.00 ($1400.00 USD) as a down payment for a printing press. This offer came at an opportune time, for the local printers were on strike and the likely outcome would be an increased cost to the customers. Father Kolbe gratefully accepted the visitor's offer and told his superiors the encouraging news.

Not long after Father Cyman's check arrived, Father Kolbe received news that the Magdalene Sisters of Lagiewnike, located near Krakow, offered to sell their old printing press for 2.5 million Polish marks. Besides Father Cyman's donation, a Father Serafino in Rome donated 30 lire, and the Franciscan community in Wilno contributed to the cause. In view of these donations, Father Kolbe's superior unexpectedly offered to put up the money for the printing press.

Operating the old press, nicknamed Granny, was physically demanding because to produce one copy, it had to be manually cranked six times. Nevertheless, not having to rely on outside printers was a great relief to Father Kolbe. He gave thanks to the Immaculate for her intercession and glorified God for granting his request.

Additional good news came along when, on January 2, 1922, Cardinal Basil Pompilii, the Vicar General of the Archdiocese of Rome, approved the Militia Immaculata as a pious union. This is the Holy See's special recognition of an organization that advances various works of piety and charity. Later that month, the first issues of *Knights of the Immaculate* were printed in-house. Publishing these 5,000 copies required 30,000 hand cranks, resulting in many bloody hands and sore backs. But Father Kolbe had proved the naysayers wrong. Soon at Grodno 6,000 copies of *The Knight* were being printed, now thirty-two pages. In addition, the friars were printing 8,000 copies of *The Seraphic Flame,* a publication of the Order of Franciscans.

This achievement was partly credited to Father Alphonse. Not only was he a gifted writer, but he turned out to be an accomplished photographer. Often he was seen walking around taking pictures of the friars steadfastly printing, addressing, and stacking the publications for shipment. His pictures were included in the publications along with advertisements encouraging young men to become members of the Franciscan Order. Seeing the friars busy working enthusiastically was an impetus to join them, and soon the monastery was crowded with new friars helping to publish more and more copies of *The Knight.*

Next, to meet the increased circulation, Father Kolbe decided to purchase a linotype machine for setting the type. Because no friar knew how to set print, Kolbe was mocked. Undeterred, he ordered the machine, trusting in Mary. Immediately after it arrived, a young man came to Grodno, asking to join the Order. He was a specialist in setting type!

At the end of the twenties, Father Kolbe was relieved of his duties as director of Militia Immaculatae by Father Melchior Fordon, a well-respected and saintly man. By then there were seventeen brothers working in Grodno with Father Kolbe. He always made sure not to ask anyone to do something that he would not do, even though he still suffered from symptoms of tuberculosis. Therefore, he was such a role model that many friars often asked to work extra hours, but he did not allow it and told them to stop asking. His intense effort in publishing the newspapers took a toll on his health and resulted in another setback. On September 26, 1926, he returned to Zokapane to rest and recover from his bout with tuberculosis. He left the operation of the printing in the capable hands of his brother, Father Alphonse.

In April of the following year, after less than full recovery, Father Kolbe was released. He was delighted to learn that the press run was up to 60,000. At that time there were 125,000 members in the Militia of the Immaculatae. Many friars still doubted their involvement in the ministry of publishing. Some of the older friars grumbled about the smell of the ink and the noises from the presses. Kolbe was in need of a larger facility to continue the printing operation. Besides, the friary at Grodno was far from where *The Knight* was distributed, which escalated expenses.

Father Kolbe decided to look for property closer to Krakow. He prayed to the Blessed Mother for her intercession and waited patiently for her to find the next location. Before long, Father Ciborowski, who happened to be visiting the Grodno friary, brought encouraging news. He told Father Kolbe that he was acquainted with a prince by the name of Jan Drucki-Lubecki, who had a large track of land about twenty-five miles from Warsaw. The visiting priest agreed to arrange a meeting for Father Maximilian and the prince so they could discuss the property.

On June 13, 1927, the meeting took place, and after a long discussion, Prince Drucki-Lubecki offered to sell his property for one million zlotys. A bit stunned, Father Kolbe said that he would inform his superiors of the offer, knowing all along that they did not have sufficient funds to purchase that property.

As a religious tactician as well as somewhat of a military strategist, Father Kolbe's first response was to go to the desired property, place a statue of the Blessed Mother on it, and pray: "Heavenly Mamusia [Mother], take possession of this land, for I know it's exactly what you desire." He reasoned that petitioning his spiritual mother was a good move. She was his strongest ally and had the most influence. Poland was devoted to her, and the prince was a member of the Militia Immaculatae. A brilliant chess player, Father Kolbe looked on his action as checkmate strategy.

After a couple of days, the prince went to the property and saw the statue of the Virgin Mary. Puzzled at first, after some thought, he concluded that Father Kolbe had set it there and that the priest sincerely wanted the land. The prince told his realtor to transfer the property without charge to the friars, for they would put it to better use than he could. When the prince gave Father Maximilian the good news, the priest profusely gave thanks to him and to the Blessed Mother.

In addition to the proposed property, Prince Lubecki donated a large plot of land. As a token of friendship and gratitude, the friars set aside a small section of it for the earthly remains, the ashes, of Prince Drucki-Lubecki. Eventually it would also be the burial site for Francis Gajowniczek, the man for whom Father Kolbe gave his life.

Father Kolbe then received permission to move all of the publishing equipment from the monastery in Grodno to the new site. He named the property Niepokalanow, Polish for City of Mary. On October 5, 1927, Father Kolbe, along with eighteen brothers, two priests, and volunteers from the surrounding neighborhoods, began building a chapel, monastery, and printing plant. Despite the harsh cold and sometimes snowy workdays, they persevered with the construction. Compassionate neighbors often brought them home-cooked meals and utensils. Tree stumps sometimes served as tables.

While the dormitories were being built, a kindly neighbor, Mrs. Jakroszewski, offered the brothers the attic of her farmhouse to use for sleeping quarters. She prepared a special bed for Father Maximilian, but holding true to his vow of poverty, he gave it to a younger, healthier brother, while he chose to sleep on wood shavings. Such humility became known throughout Poland and helped to foster new recruits of young men who wanted to follow in the footsteps of Father Kolbe and St. Francis of Assisi.

When the friars moved to the future dormitories, the beds were pallets of straw under cardboard roofs to keep some of the snow off while they slept. Brother Severyn (John) Dagis recalled the following:

> We had to get those little buildings up quickly to cover the machinery and ourselves because winter was starting. We slept on the floor—it wasn't bare ground but wood planks.

> I didn't mind that. We were young, most of us, and strong. We saw how Father Kolbe sacrificed and never complained. So how could we? After all, he was older and sick, but he was eating everything we ate, doing everything we did, and sharing our lot completely. With a leader like that, it was easy to follow.

The words of an anonymous brother describe the first meal in the friary:

> Since we had no tables, when dinnertime came, we put some planks across our suitcases and sat on the bare ground. After prayers, Father Maximilian, Father Alphonse, and fifteen of us Brothers sat at this poor table and partook of our food with Franciscan gaiety, rejoicing in what Providence sent us.

Over time, some friars decided that this austere living was too much to bear, and Father Kolbe allowed them to return to their former monastery.

On Saturday, November 12, 1927, Father Kolbe celebrated the first Mass on this site as the construction continued. Shortly after, the printing plant and the electrical power station were complete and ready for full operation. Father Alphonse and eighteen friars arrived in Niepokalanow from Grodno to begin their new assignments.

As word spread about Niepokalanow, the amount of incoming mail grew every week. Because of this and the number of publications printed each week, a spur of the railroad going to Warsaw had to be built. No doubt, this was most pleasing to the friars and, most importantly, to the Blessed Mother. A minor seminary was also planned for Niepokolanow. Finally, on

September 16, 1929, thirty students were welcomed into it to begin their studies and discernment for becoming Franciscan priests.

By 1930, buildings housing the administration, the printing presses, and the dormitories for the friars and seminarians were completed. By this time, 340,000 copies of *The Knight* were being distributed and membership in the M.I. was steadily rising. Father Kolbe's dreams were blossoming, and the first City of Mary had come together. Now he focused on the rest of the world with an eye to the heavily populated Far East.

Chapter 8

Mission to the Orient

Once when Father Kolbe was on a train, he met some Japanese students and was impressed by their kindness. A desire to bring them the Good News of Jesus was born in his heart. He asked his superior, Father Cornelius Czupryk, for permission to build a City of Mary in Japan. In view of Kolbe's past incredible successes against all odds, this next daring venture was approved. Father Czupryk gave the following account:

> He came in before noon and asked me to permit him to go to the Orient. . . . I was taken aback.
>
> "Where will you live? What will you do?"
>
> "The Blessed Mother has her plan ready," was his answer.
>
> "Who'll take your place here?"
>
> He said his brother, whom I knew was a capable person and talented editor, would take his place. I told him I'd have to think it over, consult with others, and then I'd decide. Those I consulted did not approve heartily. First he was ill, and second he didn't even know exactly where he was going. . . . Still, Maximilian had this gift: when he proposed anything, he did it so clearly, with such conviction and strong faith, that it was difficult for me to opposed his request. So in the end, I agreed. I took the decision upon myself. I told him, however, to go by way of the Father General in Rome, convinced that there he would be sent back.

Prior to leaving for Japan, Father Maximilian gathered all of the friars at the City of Mary and celebrated his last Mass for some time to come. After the final blessing at Mass, the friars convened in front of the statue of the Blessed Mother that he and

Father Alphonse had erected on the property. He bid a sad farewell to the City of Mary, which he and his friars had devoted days and nights to build. Then he and Brothers Zeno, Hilary, Severyn (John), and Zygmund departed, not knowing when or if they would be back.

As the friars crossed France, they stopped at Lourdes and Lisieux. On Wednesday, February 26, 1930, the missionaries took the train to Marseilles and then boarded the freighter Angers. Freighters were Father Kolbe's transportation of choice as it was the cheapest, reinforcing his title of "God's Miser." The group traveled across the Red Sea, down the Indian Ocean, and entered the China Sea. Except for some bouts of seasickness that a couple of the friars suffered, everyone arrived safely in their first destination, Shanghai, China, anxious to begin their ministry in a new and challenging environment.

First on the agenda for Thursday, April 24, 1930, was meeting with Auxiliary Bishop Monsignor Auguste Haouissee at his office in Shanghai. At that time missionaries in China were assigned to specific provinces based on the 1926 Chinese Catholic Congress. The five Conventual Franciscans were sent to a remote area of China, making it unlikely that they would be able to do any publishing. The bishop did not fully comprehend Father Maximilian's intentions and devotion to the Blessed Mother, so he was not inclined to give permission to publish. He did, however, authorize the friars to distribute copies of *The Knight.*

Providentially, Father Kolbe met a millionaire by the name of Joseph-Lo-Pa-Hong. The man's family, whose Catholicism went back three centuries, was attracted to the Franciscans' devotion to the poor. Because of his admiration of Father Maximilian and the friars, the wealthy man graciously offered them a house for their friary. Now that the missionaries had a place to call their own, Brothers Severlyn and Zymund remained in China to carry on their work. Father Kolbe and the other two brothers continued on their journey to Japan.

On the afternoon of April 24, 1930, the three missionaries arrived safely in Ohato, the port terminal of Nagasaki. Their first order of business after disembarking was to take a taxi to the city of Oura, about a one-mile drive from the harbor. There at the top of a steep hill they saw the Oura cathedral, built in 1853. To the right of it was Bishop Hayasake's residence and the seminary. The Franciscans walked up the hill and were drawn to a beautiful statue of the Virgin Mary, prominently located in front of the cathedral. Father Maximilian immediately felt at peace, as if Mary were right there welcoming him and his friars to Japan. The missionaries knelt and prayed in front of the statue, thanking their Blessed Mother for their safe arrival and praying for success in their missionary endeavors. Then they proceeded to the bishop's residence, where they were afforded a cordial Japanese welcome.

Father Kolbe explained to Bishop Hayasake the group's purposes for coming to his country. The bishop was especially interested in Father Kolbe's zeal for promoting devotion to the Immaculate Mary and listened intently as Father told of his yearning to set up a printing press in order to publish *The Knight.* He explained that he aimed not only to reach out to the Catholic population of Japan but to evangelize others. Initially the bishop was not in favor of having him set up a printing press, believing that this was a bit too ambitious and unrealistic. Undeterred, Kolbe informed Bishop Hayasake that he had doctorates in theology and philosophy. As he pulled out his diploma, the bishop smiled and then laughed, saying, "While I was many miles away begging the Dominicans for a professor of philosophy, one was seated on my doorstep. All right, Father Maximilian, if I may have my professor, you may have your journal."

With permission granted and upon consultation with his counselors, Father Kolbe began teaching at the seminary and established the *Rycerz Niepolkalanej* magazine in Japan. Unfortunately, he suffered some serious health problems stemming from exposure to the new climate, an oriental diet that did not agree with him, and symptoms associated with tuberculosis.

Among his medical issues were boils, headaches, chills, terrible tremors, and fevers. He became so weak that when saying Mass, he had to be held up by his fellow brothers. Asked by his doctors how he managed, he simply said that by continuous prayer, especially the Rosary, he was able to attain mystical union with God.

As Father Kolbe taught theology at the seminary, the other two friars set up and printed the first issue of *The Knight* in Japanese. Through divine providence, a devout Methodist and school teacher, Tagita Koyo, was so impressed with Father Kolbe's charisma that he not only helped with the translation but also recruited a friend, Mr. Yamaka, who was staunchly anti-Catholic, to translate. When Mr. Yamaka attacked the Catholic faith, Mr. Koyo fiercely defended it and eventually converted to Catholicism.

Miraculously, against all odds and despite the bishop's expectations, on May 24 the first edition of *Seibo No Kishi* (The Knight of Mary Without Sin) was sent out, with thanks to the Immaculata. By 1933, *The Knight* had a circulation of 50,000 and was the largest publication in Japan at the time.

While celebrating the success of their publication and growing apostolate, the friars also had to deal with a problem—the lack of space. Their quarters were inadequate especially during the winter as Father Kolbe related in a letter home: "Heavy snow fell last night. To sleep we had to cover our heads as the snow was hitting our faces. In the morning our dormitory was absolutely white . . . and the basins full of ice." Another friar added, "We're sleeping on straw . . . we eat from benches and sit on the ground. The poverty is extreme but we are very happy."

Dr. Jacob Yasuro Fukahori was astonished when X-rays revealed how serious Father Kolbe's tuberculosis was. The doctor often tried to persuade him to go to a sanatorium, but the friar preferred to work. During bad spells, he would stay in bed for a few days.

One night Father Kolbe became so ill that he summoned one of the other friars to his side and asked him to tell the brothers to stick close to the Blessed Mother if he should die. By midnight, he survived his illness and continued on with his mission. However, the relief and joy of his recovery were dashed by the news that Father Alphonse Kolbe had died from a ruptured appendix on December 3, 1930, in Warsaw. The telegram, which arrived in Japan five days later, came as a shock because Father Alphonse was only thirty-four years old and the editor of *The Knight.*

On hearing this dreadful news, Father Kolbe felt lonely and pondered whether he should remain in Japan. He also wondered who, if anyone, could replace his brother, such a talented writer and editor, and how his death would affect the mission at Niepokalanow. Kolbe acknowledged that he and his brother had disagreements over various matters concerning their mission and the newspaper, but they had overcome them and were moving forward. He recalled the last correspondence he received from Father Alphonse, dated Thursday, September 18, 1930: "Don't fear, apart from poverty no evil threatens us. I myself see ever more clearly and increasingly recognize what Niepokalanow is, and I convince myself that I really know very little."

To celebrate his brother's life, Father Maximilian donned his white vestment, signifying resurrection, and celebrated a Requiem Mass for Father Alphonse's soul. Wasting no time, he wrote a letter to Father Florian Koziura the next day, appointing him to replace Father Alphonse as the publisher and editor of *The Knight.* In the letter he reiterated that St. Francis was their model for their mission, which was to bring salvation and sanctification to souls. As part of that mission they were to continue to live in poverty as St. Francis did, for this was "an inexhaustible treasury of divine providence."

Toward the end of 1930, seeing how the circulation of *Seibo no Kishi* was climbing, Kolbe began to think about finding another piece of land in order to expand the friars' presence in Japan. Property where the friars were living was expensive, so finding land nearby was out of the question. Because the lease on their property would expire at the end of January 1931, a decision had to be made fairly quickly. In a letter, the Father Provincial told him that if he found a suitable piece of land and the price was reasonable, then he could purchase it.

Father Kolbe found property in the Hongochi district about three miles from the center of Nagasaki, but some friars had concerns. The land was on the slope of Mount Hikosan (meaning "Echo Mountain"), so a considerable amount of terracing would be required. Moreover, it was near a burial ground, regarded as superstitious in Japanese culture. However, the friars could purchase the three-acre site for $3500. At the same time, Brother Zeno found a location that was more suitable for constructing a building, not to mention it was closer to the largest Catholic population of Nagasaki. However, conversions to Christ and not ministering to the existing population of Catholics was foremost in Father Kolbe's mind. He pictured the morning sun rising over the mountains, shining on beautifully terraced slopes. This vision, along with a prayerful heart and trust in divine providence, was enough to convince him that the less expensive property, although requiring more work, was the right place for the Japanese version of Niepokalanow.

Father Kolbe made the right choice, no doubt due to the Blessed Mother and her Son watching over the friars. On March 4, 1931, he finalized the purchase. As it turned out, had he built his new monastery in Nagasaki as Brother Zeno suggested, the atomic bomb dropped on that city on August 6, 1945, ending World War II, would have destroyed the monastery and killed all those who lived and worked there. The chosen site was on the other side of the mountain, which provided a protective barrier from the bomb's destruction. This resulted in no major damage to the property or serious injuries to those who occupied the monastery. The friars took in abandoned children there and founded an orphanage that eventually housed a thousand children. Today, U.S. sailors from the Sasebo Naval Base often travel to the orphanage to contribute their time and money in assisting Franciscans and the children.

Once the Franciscans owned the new property, Father Kolbe assigned Brother Zeno the responsibility of hiring an architect and other contractors and overseeing the construction. Father Kolbe carried on his primary duties of writing and publishing the *Seibo no Kishi* during much of the day. Then in the late afternoon and early evening, he joined the other friars in manual labor at the construction site.

After two months of intensive labor, the site was ready for the construction crews to frame the walls and roof. True to their vows of poverty and simplicity, the friars chose the standard low-cost materials for their buildings: wood and mud. Brother Zeno contracted with carpenters from the local Hongochi community for the interior construction, but that created some contentious moments. Unbeknownst to Brother Zeno, there was historic competition in the construction business between Hongoshi laborers and others referred to as "urban aliens" as to who would do structural work. This competition led to some feuding, but in the end the problem was resolved. The friars learned another lesson in their new missionary territory.

On May 16, 1931, Father Kolbe decided that the building was finished to the point that the friars could occupy it. He named it *Mugenzai no Sono*, Garden of the Immaculata. While no doubt he was pleased that Japan had its own version of Niepokalanow rising up from the slope of Mount Hikosan and overlooking the non-Christian district of Hongonchi, the building had many issues. For example, the roof of cement tiles was not weatherproof, and the thin walls allowed weather, mosquitoes and other insects inside. Brother Bart recalled, "The humidity was so intense that first you worked in your habit—that's all we had—soaked with sweat. Then when you washed the thing and hung it out, it wouldn't dry."

For Father Kolbe and his stouthearted missionaries, such living conditions were not much different from what they tolerated when they built and occupied the buildings of Niepokalanow in Poland. Laboring often in harsh weather and lacking most creature comforts some other religious orders enjoyed, they accepted them as part of their vowed life, just as their founder St. Francis did in his time; and, like him, they did it with joy.

Several months later when construction was complete, a statue of the Blessed Mother was placed high atop the property. It was the crowning touch of the accomplishment of the friars' long and arduous labor of love. They were now ready to go out into their new community and evangelize those who did not know the true joy of the Gospel of Jesus Christ.

While Father Kolbe and the friars were working on their new building project in Japan, things were literally heating up in Niepokalanow. The friars there experienced their first fire since the monastery opened. It occurred in the new power plant. The friars ran to the well, filled buckets with water, and successfully extinguished the fire, but not before serious damage was done to their generators.

After the fire, Father Kolbe, who was notified of it, and Father Florian Koziura, the Guardian (superior) at Niepokalanow, realized it was time to form a fire brigade there. They selected several friars to become the first firefighters and provided them with the skills to be prepared for the next fire. Finally, on July 2, 1931, the group trained officially became the Volunteer Fire Brigade of Niepokalanow. During their dedication, the friars invoked the intercession of St. Florian, a fourth-century saint who was the patron of firefighters. Next, a firetruck was purchased. Because of the support many in the local community had given ever since the monastery was founded, the friars extended their firefighting services to adjacent communities, including Teresin, Paprotinia, and Szmanow, and became renowned for their services. To this day the Niepokalanow Volunteer Fire Brigade continues to serves these communities.

A year after the friars moved into their new monastery in Japan, Father Kolbe believed that it was time to travel to another country and expand his mission. So, in May of 1932, he boarded a boat from the docks of Nagaskai and traveled to India, making stops in Hong Kong and Singapore along the way. He never let his tuberculosis and other maladies deter his desire to conquer other territories on behalf of Christ and his Mother, who had always been the driving forces behind his missionary life.

Finally, in early July, after several weeks of journeying across the high seas, Father Kolbe boarded a train to the city of Ernakulum, Ceylon (now Sri Lanka). On the train, he had a chance encounter with a Syrian priest and seized the opportunity to educate him about the M.I. and the purpose of his trip. The Syrian priest provided a brief history lesson, informing Father Kolbe that India was separated into two missionary zones, one overseen by an order from the Syrian Rite and the other by a Roman Rite order. He cautioned Father Kolbe not to be optimistic about establishing a mission there because the archbishop might not welcome a third missionary order. The kindly priest offered Father Kolbe a room at his residence for the night, because it was probably the most comfortable one in the city. Father Kolbe gratefully accepted it as a welcome relief after his long and sometimes rough journey across the sea.

After a restful night, the two priests traveled to the residence of Archbishop Angelus Maria Perez Cecilia. There a Carmelite priest, an aide to the archbishop, informed them that he was not there that day and inquired the nature of Father Kolbe's business. Father Kolbe explained that the friars in Poland and Japan wanted to expand the Militia Immaculatae to include India and produce a journal in hopes of winning more souls to Christ through the Blessed Mother. The aide responded that Father Kolbe should not have much hope because, despite his impressive credentials, a third missionary order was unlikely. But he went on to say that the archbishop would return the next day and be glad to see him then.

The following day Father Kolbe returned to the chancery and joined the line of others scheduled to meet with the archbishop. As he waited, he noticed a statue of St. Thérèse of Lisieux, to whom he had a special devotion. He had prayed for her canonization, which occurred in 1925. On her deathbed, St. Thérèse promised to spend heaven doing good on earth and send down a shower of roses. Father Kolbe began praying for her intercession in regard to his mission effort. Oddly enough, as he finished his prayer, a rose petal from the wreath on her head fell and landed by his foot. He said to himself, "Let's see what this means."

When Father Kolbe was received into the archbishop's office, he explained the history of the M.I. movement and told him that the friars had established a mission in Japan. To Father Kolbe's surprise and delight, the archbishop said, "Come, Father, come! Establish your order here and help us to convert the population to Christianity."

If that were not enough good news, Archbishop Perez promised Father Kolbe a residence, a chapel, and another building near a railroad station. Perhaps this was an affirmation of the saint's holiness and the power of his voice in procuring truly unexpected gifts.

While Father Kolbe was most thankful and happy at receiving this good news, it would be many years before his friars would see it come to fruition. This was due to a shortage of qualified missionaries coupled with the fact that Poland restricted the export of its currency, so funds couldn't be sent to India to support the mission. Nevertheless, for Father Kolbe, the permission was a victory for the Immaculata.

Leaving India on a boat for the journey back to Japan, Father Kolbe had high hopes of returning to India in the near future. Unfortunately, those hopes were dashed by World War II and his continuing health problems. Not until May 10, 1981, in the town of Chotty, Karala, would a mission outpost be opened in India by Franciscans when two Maltese finally fulfilled Father Kolbe's dream.

Back at the mission in Hongochi, Father Kolbe spent the next six months guiding the friars in their expanding mission work, all the while enduring the daily challenges of the Japanese climate and food in addition to his health issues.

Chapter 9

Progress and Radio Niepokalanow

On April 7, 1933, Father Kolbe left Nagasaki by boat for Krakow in order to attend the Franciscan Provincial Chapter, a mandatory meeting. As he was departing from the Land of the Rising Sun, events elsewhere had unfolded that year that would ultimately have a major impact not only on Father Kolbe and his missionary work but on the world at large.

On January 30, German president Paul von Hindenburg had appointed Adolph Hitler, who was leader of the National Socialist German Workers Party (Nazi party), as the new chancellor of Germany. The following month Japan suddenly announced its withdrawal from the League of Nations, leaving the world in shock. Japan had been a key component in the League of Nations in helping to maintain peace and reducing the risk of another world war. Then in March, Franklin Delano Roosevelt became the thirty-second president of the United States, making him the commander-in-chief of the military. In 1939, Germany would invade Poland and go on to occupy France and attack England. While all of Europe was vulnerable, Poland was specifically under the tyranny of German rule.

When Father Kolbe arrived back at Niepokalanow, the friars gave him a warm and cheerful reception, applauding him for establishing the Garden of the Immaculate in Nagasaki and publishing *The Knight* in Japanese. Despite the accolades paid to the beloved founder, during the meeting questions and controversy arose among the community leaders as to whether to continue the apostolic work in Japan. With a bowed head, Father Kolbe fervently prayed to the Blessed Mother while he listened to the debate. The Father Provincial suggested voting to abandon the mission in Japan, obviously a disappointment to Father Kolbe. The votes were cast. The friars agreed that the mission should continue, to the delight of the humble priest who founded it.

The Provincial Chapter also determined that Father Kolbe needed time away from Japan to recuperate from tuberculosis. Another vote was cast to choose a replacement for him as superior of the Japan mission. When the votes were tallied, Father Cornelius Czupryk was elected. An additional vote was taken that resulted in a decision to send Father Kolbe back some day, but without the responsibilities of superior.

First, Father Kolbe began a period of bedrest to recuperate from tuberculosis and exhaustion from the long hours working at the Japanese mission. Not one for sitting around and doing nothing, he took advantage of his enforced rest to write and edit articles for *The Knight.* Nothing, included his health, deterred him from spreading the knowledge and love for the Mother of Jesus to others. He never forgot his encounter with Mary at age ten when she offered him two crowns. He received the white crown of chastity when he became a priest. He now looked forward to the red crown of martyrdom.

On Tuesday, October 3, 1933, Father Kolbe, along with Father Cornelius Czupryk, voyaged to Japan. On their arrival at Mugenzai no Sono, they received an enthusiastic welcome from the friars. For three years progress had been made. The number of friars had increased to forty-five. This included eighteen boys in the minor seminary (the equivalent of junior high school), one in the major seminary, and four Japanese seminarians. Also two priests and eighteen brothers from Poland had joined the mission.

Despite the warring factions escalating all over Europe and Japan, the friars pursued their duties at the Nagasaki mission. Father Kolbe continued to teach at the seminary, write and edit the Japanese *The Knight,* and act as general administrator of the M.I. for the friars in Japan. Meanwhile, growth continued in Niepokolanow. On April 4, 1935, the first issue of the *Informator RN* was published for the benefit of those in the inner circles of the M.I. in Poland. The following month, under the editorship of Father Marian Wojcik, the friars began publishing the *Maly Dziennik* (Small Daily Newspaper). This was a wish come true for the Polish bishops who for many years wanted a newspaper that reported on current events within the Polish Catholic community. In the new newspaper were stories about activities in parish churches, upcoming conferences for the clergy, and political updates. Information about the world outside of Poland was particularly critical because Poland was surrounded by countries preparing for war and keeping current would help the bishops deal with whatever happened.

Father Kolbe always had a special zeal for spreading his Catholic faith, especially love of the Blessed Mother. To accomplish this, he stayed on the cutting edge of the latest communication technology. Informing his fellow friars and everyone he could reach with news of the latest current events, along with inspiring articles proclaiming truth and the good news of the Gospels, was always foremost in his mind. This long-held passion was one of the hallmarks of his priesthood.

While things were going well inside the Garden of Mary, such was not the case beyond its walls. Japan's army was invading and occupying parts of China, and Hitler's army was beginning its historic march into Europe.

Another Provincial Chapter was called in 1936, and Father Czupryk and Father Kolbe were going to attend. Before they left, Father Kolbe spoke these prophetic words to the friars: "I would like to suffer and die in a knightly manner, even shedding blood if it will hasten the day when the whole world acknowledges Mary as the Immaculate Mother of God."

The two priests were welcomed back to the City of Niepokalanow. The friars always looked upon Father Kolbe as a father and admired and respected him as their founder. By then the population of the seminary had increased to one hundred seventy-five students, fifty-six seminarians, two hundred ninety-five brothers, and thirteen priests. Even more pleasing to Father Kolbe was the fact that the circulation of *The Knight* had climbed to more than 600,000. When he was praised for this accomplishment, his humility was such that he gave all the acclaim to the Blessed Mother, whose intercession he said made it possible.

The Franciscan Provincial Chapter met from July 12 to July 16. During it, Father Kolbe was appointed Guardian of Niepokalanow. This ruled out his returning to Japan and confirmed a premonition he had recently experienced. The chapter further appointed Father Samuel Rosenbaiger as the new Guardian of Mugenzai no Sono mission in Japan in place of Kolbe.

Once the chapter meeting had concluded, Father Kolbe went to work expanding the M.I. to several other European countries. He believed they were fertile territory, and he always acted on his intuitions as the inspiration of the Holy Spirit. Among his initiatives were an Italian edition of *The Knight,* a Polish magazine for children, and even a supplement paper on sports.

During this time, Father Kolbe was feeling somewhat apprehensive about the finances of the mission in Nagasaki. He circumvented the Polish regulation preventing the export of currency to certain countries by transferring money to Japan from Franciscan accounts in other countries, such as Belgium, France, Denmark, and Czechoslovakia. In addition, Father Rosenbaiger toured a number of dioceses in the United States, pleading for financial assistance. The generosity of many Catholics there provided the much needed financial stability for the Japanese mission. The indomitable faith of the M.I. friars brought about these answers to their prayers.

December 8, 1937, was the tenth anniversary of the founding of the city of Niepokalanow and its monastery. The city's formation had begun with only 6 brothers. It now had 10 priests, 537 brothers, and 16 novices. The minor seminary comprised 136 students. Amazingly, a total of 33,872 people were members of the M.I. Among other encouraging statistics were the following:

- 754,000 copies of *Rycerz Niepokalanej* were printed in December.
- 693,000 calendars were printed.

- 173,000 copies of *The Little Knight* were in circulation.
- 130,000 copies of *Maly Dziennik* were printed daily along with the weekend edition of 223,270 copies.
- 730 copies of *Niepokalanow Information* were printed.
- 775,847 pieces of mail were received by the editorial staff during December.

Brothers worked in shifts so that the mission was carried out almost twenty-four hours a day. How could Father Kolbe, his fellow friars, and a host of lay followers of this humble priest not be overwhelmed with joy and excitement by so many accomplishments, made possible through the miracle of donations procured by begging—a timeless trait of missionary work?

In celebrating the tenth anniversary, Father Kolbe addressed the people of Poland on Polish National Radio. Over the course of his broadcast, he explained the philosophy behind the founding of the M.I. and the establishment of the monastery. He also presented the history of the doctrine of the Immaculate Conception of the Blessed Mother, which traces its roots to the beginnings of the Catholic Church. He recounted the story of the Blessed Mother's apparition in 1858 at Lourdes, France, when she identified herself to Bernadette as the Immaculate Conception and gave the world the message to pray and do penance. Father Kolbe also informed his listeners about his early years of begging on the streets and in churches and how the experience and struggle made him a much humbler priest. He said that he had to remind himself that he was begging not for himself but for the Immaculata and for souls. During the talk, he told the story of the miraculous provision of 500 marks, the exact amount owed the printer in 1922. He also highlighted the accomplishments and conversions over the past ten years and stated that all were owing to his spiritual mother, the friars, and members of the M.I.

By 1938, Poland had a population of about 34 million people, and editions of *The Knight* were being distributed to more than one million households. After reading their copies, people would forward them to others, thereby covering a significant portion of Poland. The spiritual Militia in Poland alone totaled 691,219, and several hundred thousand members were located in the Far East and other countries served by the Conventual Franciscans.

Not only were the friars spiritually gifted, but they had multiple talents, which Father Kolbe encouraged them to develop to the maximum. Obviously, the Franciscans had expertise in writing and printing. They also had a facility for learning foreign languages. Brother Severyn (John) Dagis, for example, in record time learned to typeset the four thousand signs in the Japanese alphabet. He produced the first Japanese publication typeset by a European. Other brothers had unique aptitudes. One brother was a master watchmaker and wrote several authoritative works on the subject. Another brother was a dentist. When Father Kolbe had an airstrip built at Niepokalanow in order to distribute the publications to a wider area and more effectively, several friars became pilots.

Father Kolbe's interest in communications and expertise in science were manifested early. When he was thirteen years old, he invented a form of telegraphic communications similar to a telex. Although his idea never went beyond the drawing board, it testified to his intellectual ability and hinted at his tenacity in following his dream of using the most modern and effective tools to promote the faith. It's no surprise that Father Kolbe said, "If Jesus or St. Francis were alive now, they'd use modern technology to reach the people." He saw state-of-the-art technology as a means to spread his message about the Blessed Mother and bring the Gospel of Christ to a larger audience.

Radio was coming into vogue, a way to communicate with a worldwide audience. While continuing to improve and expand the use of print media as his primary method of communicating, Father Kolbe already had applied to the Polish government for a radio license in 1930. At that time, however, licenses were only granted to Radio Warsaw, the Polish military, and amateur radio operators. Since 1924, even radio receivers were only allowed to those who had permission from the government. Father Kolbe's application was rejected, but he would continue to pursue this advanced form of communication.

While stationed in Japan, Father Kolbe became acquainted with a network of local radio stations that reenergized his desire to utilize the new medium to reach beyond the limits of his publications about the Militia Immaculatae. Between his talk on Polish National Radio in 1937 and a sermon broadcast on February 2, 1938, he sent Brother Manswet Marczewski to the Warsaw amateur radio club to take a radio course. After this brother successfully completed the course, Father Kolbe pursued and was granted a permit for construction and operation of a radio station. On October 26, 1938, the project began, and Kolbe addressed the friars with these words: "Remember, the purpose of every effort is to disseminate the faith by the written word, the spoken word, and perhaps someday through producing films."

While the building and antenna were being constructed, the Walter Company in Warsaw was building a transmitter. Once the transmitter was installed at Niepokalanow, it was immediately upgraded to enhance its signal. Finally, in December of 1938, Father Kolbe was given oral permission to test the transmitting station. He chose the call sign SP3RN. The SP3 was the amateur radio prefix for Poland, and RN stood for Radio Niepokalanow. The following message was transmitted on the forty-meter band on December 8, 1938: "This station [Sp3RN] can be found on your receivers outside the Polish amateur radio band 41.4m, between 41.1 and 41.4m; . . . Allegedly there are 50,000 amateur radio operators. Some will listen out of curiosity, others out of sadness."

The Radio Niepokalanow station worked on the day of the Immaculate Conception and the Sunday after only based on oral permission. Transmissions had to be suspended until a written license was issued. A full broadcast license was not issued before

World War II. Radio Niepokalanow was the first Catholic radio station in Poland. It is now a commercial radio station.

Father Maximilian was also aware of the inception of television but knew that this medium was not ready for him to implement. No doubt, this progressive priest, who was never satisfied with the status quo, would have made good use of it to spread the Gospel.

Chapter 10

The Invasion and War

On March 2, 1939, the Catholic world heralded a new pope. Vatican Secretary of State Eugenio Cardinal Pacelli was elected by the College of Cardinals to ascend to the papacy and chose the name Pius XII. His nineteen-year reign was a tumultuous one. His efforts to persuade world leaders to avoid war were in vain. Despite his stance against Nazism and his statements condemning race-based persecutions, he was criticized for not being more outspoken in regard to the atrocities of the Nazi Germany concentration camps. This pope's perceived silence would be a controversial matter and mar his legacy.

No sooner had Pius XII assumed office than the world witnessed the beginning stages of World War II. After annexing Austria, on March 6, Hitler's army marched into Prague, Czechoslovakia, and promptly dismantled and abolished the country. At this juncture it became obvious that none of the surrounding countries, especially Poland, would be capable of stopping the Germany army.

As the drums of war were beginning to beat all around Poland, the friars at Niepokalanow prepared for the inevitability of war. At a mission conference Father Maximilian attended in Berlin in March of 1938, he became aware of a new Kulturkampf. The German word meaning "culture struggle" originated in the 1870s when there was a power struggle between Germany and the Roman Catholic Church that culminated when the German government resisted Vatican Council I's dogma on papal infallibility.

Based on what Father Kolbe learned at the conference, he was convinced that in all likelihood Hitler would implement Blitzkrieg (lightning war) in Poland. This military maneuver with armored vehicles and air support used speed and surprise to generate disorganization within the defending country. Because Poland had no natural borders to withstand the thrust of invading armies, not to mention that its military consisted of only small cavalry units, it appeared only a matter of time before Niepokalanow would be face to face with Hitler's panzers.

Armed with the latest intelligence on an impending war with Germany, Father Kolbe returned to Niepokalanow and immediately gathered the friars and informed them of the recent reports of an invasion and what to expect. As a true patriot of Poland, he wanted the friars to support the Polish force as much as they could under the rules of their order, which did not allow the use of funds for aggressive commitments. Given his limited options, he chose to allocate to the Polish forces money the friars normally spent on sugar, a special treat. He justified this as necessary for defensive purposes since Poland was not the aggressor.

Another important item on the pre-war agenda was to prepare for the expected German attack. The friars' windows and building openings were to be shielded to block interior light so that if German aircraft were headed their way, their buildings would not be spotted. The friars installed an air raid siren on the grounds. One night during choir practice Father Kolbe had an unannounced air raid drill. However, the music and voices prevented the friars from hearing the siren. Father Kolbe bolted through the door to see the choir singing and no one reacting to the siren. Disappointed and upset, he yelled, "How can you disregard the drill?" The startled friars immediately suspended their choir practice and scurried around covering up the windows and other openings. Kolbe bid the friars goodnight and reconsidered his decision to hold unscheduled drills.

By this time, Father Kolbe had become a household name and a hero not only to the Catholic faithful throughout Poland but in other European countries, Japan, and India. He had developed a reputation as a great communicator through the eleven Catholic newspapers and periodicals produced daily by the friars of M.I. He instilled faith and trust through his words and actions at a time when it was most needed. The astute friar that he was, Kolbe had become an outspoken critic of the Nazis and the communists. He once addressed his friars with this message:

> A frightful struggle is coming. Here in Poland we can expect the worst. We need not worry, but must bravely conform our will to the will of Mary Immaculate. The physical sufferings will only help toward making us holier. We should even thank those who torment us. A soft word to hard hearts may convert them. In short, we are invincible.

On Thursday, July 27, 1939, Father Maximilian and Father Marian joined others involved in the Polish media at the foreign office in Warsaw for the latest briefing on the buildup of German forces. Another purpose was to urge them to encourage their readers to intensify their patriotic efforts as war loomed. One delegate had the following message:

> Tell your readers that they must be prepared for every sacrifice to save the nation. We have every reason to believe that Hitler will seek to continue his dismantling of the Versailles Treaty by reclaiming the Soilesia region and the city of Gdansk and by incorporating the Polish corridor in the new German State. The Versailles Treaty, which Germany always despised, helped bring an end to World War I and recreated the Polish nation. Hitler's foreign policy goal is to destroy that treaty and with it the Polish nation.

A month later, on August 23, the news reported the signing of a Friendship Nonaggression Pact between Poland's two archenemies, Germany and Russian. Under the provisions of Article 4, it stated: "Neither of the two contracting parties will join any group of powers which is directed, mediately, or immediately against the other party." This was simply a conspiratorial pact to destroy the nation of Poland, but came as no surprise to Father Kolbe and his brother friars.

On hearing of this pact, the friars asked Father Kolbe how it could be possible. He explained as follows:

> It's possible because the pact is directed against Poland. Two of the tyrants of our past history who kept our nation partitioned for more than a century now plan to divide our country once again. As your ancestors did, we must resist the destruction of our state. As they resisted the rule of Prussia and Russia, we must resist the rule of godless Bolshevism and the idols of an Aryan National Socialism. Prepared for every sacrifice, let us entrust ourselves and our nation into the maternal care of the Immaculata, Poland's Queen. Beloved Children, we can be confident that, if we do not survive the imminent storm, the Immaculata will not forget her people and her nation which fervently petition her.

These words of the founder left no question about the seriousness of the situation. It was simply a matter of time before war would commence, and no one knew who among the friars would survive and who would not. The mystic friar and founder of Niepokalanow, Father Kolbe, intuitively knew he would soon bear a cross for his dearly beloved Poland and the Immaculate. The road he would travel would culminate in sainthood.

That same month Father Kolbe and Brother Hieronim saw a prophetic sign in the sky over the friary. As they were leaving the refectory (dining room), they observed in the northern sky a white cross against a deep purple background. Almost instantaneously, the sky changed to a flaming red. The sight lasted for a mere few seconds. Brother Hieronim, who died on August 4, 2001, said during an interview with Claude R. Foster, as quoted in his book *Mary's Knight* (pp.561-582): "This celestial phenomenon would prove to be the harbinger of the titanic struggle about to begin: a nation, under its banner of red and white, fighting for survival, and a Franciscan priest, Maksymilian Maria Kolbe—the personification of martyrdom—about to receive the red cross promised him in his youth."

On September 1, 1939, at about 5:45 AM, Nazi planes dropped bombs on the tiny town of Wielun, Poland, signaling the dawn of World War II in Europe. This small city in central Poland had no military targets. The attack took the lives of approximately 1,300 civilians and injured hundreds more. Later that day Adolph Hitler announced to the German Reichstag (Parliament) and to Germany that World War II had begun.

As soon as Father Kolbe got word of the attack on Wielun, he directed the friars to burn all copies of *Maly Dziennik.* This religious publication was critical of the Nazis' pagan ideology. If it landed in German hands, the friars' lives would be in danger.

After discerning the next step to take in anticipation of the imminent invasion of German troops, Father Kolbe brought together all of the members of the Niepoklalanow community on September 5, 1939. He made farewell remarks, gave his final blessings, and informed them of his plan to disperse most of them to other places. He told them of his deep regret for having to evacuate them and reassured them that they would be under the safe protection of the Blessed Mother, although some would not survive the war, including him. He went on to say the following:

> Some of you will volunteer to serve in the Polish Red Cross. Others can serve wherever they're needed in hospitals, in clinics or wherever a ministry to the ill, wounded, and dying can be conducted. Some will return home to family. Remember, Niepokalanow is not only a building and machinery. The genuine Niepokalanow is you. Niepokalanow is wherever you are. The City of the Immaculata is your mission of love to neighbor and to the world. As the Apostle to the Gentiles wrote to the Corinthians: "You are our letter, written on our hearts,

> known and read by all . . . written not in ink but by the Spirit of the living God, not on the tablets of stone but on tablets that are hearts of flesh." In ministering to souls, all of whom the Immaculata loves and seeks to win for her son, you represent Niepokalanow and the Militia Immaculatae. Wherever you go, in all that you do, don't forget love, for if we do not perform God's truth, we cannot possess it, and God's truth obligates us to love.

By the conclusion of his talk, tears were flowing from all in attendance, a testament of their undying love for their founder. This would be the last time most of them would see him, for 13 priests, 622 brothers, 15 novices and 122 students in the minor seminary would leave. Only 36 brothers, Father Pius Bartosik and Ludwig Kim, a Korean cleric, would stay behind. Some of these had no other place to go and wanted to keep the monastery open to serve the Niepokalanow community and people outside the monastery. Others simply wanted to remain with their founder and support him no matter the circumstances.

After dispersing the friars to their new assignments, Father Kolbe drove to Warsaw for a personal meeting with the Father Provincial, Father Maurycy Madzurek. As the conversation began, Kolbe reported on the evacuation and those remaining behind. He went on to explain the importance of maintaining the fire brigade and the air raid siren, both of which benefited the entire area.

"Very well," said the Father Provincial, "as long as the brothers know that we cannot guarantee their safety in the friary. The world has become victim to demonic forces when security can't be found even in a monastery. You know, do you not, that your editor of *Maly Dziennik,* Father Marian, and also your benefactor, Prince Drucki-Lubecki, have fled Poland?"

Father Kolbe, who had a passport and could go to Italy, asked what he should do. The Father Provincial told him to return to Niepokalanow. Without protest, Father Kolbe obeyed. He would continue his role as the shepherd guarding his flock from the armies of Germany and the Soviet Union.

Back at Niepokalanow, one of Father Kolbe's first tasks was to shave off his beard, which he grew in Japan. As part of his cultural orientation, he had learned that within the Japanese business community a beard was a sign of prestige and learning. Now in Poland it could be deemed provocative, especially when coupled with wearing a habit, which was a requirement of the order. After Brother Kamil shaved off the beard, he placed strands of hair in a pouch. Now on display at St. Maximilian Kolbe's museum in Niepolalanow, this is the only first class relic of the saint.

That same day, bombs hit the railroad station at Szymano filled with refugees who had fled from Poznan and western Poland. The neighboring communities of Teresin, Szymanow, and Paporotnia were rocked by the explosions, and some of the monastery buildings a few hundred yards from the station shuddered. The brothers immediately ran to the railroad station to assist those who were injured and dying. Following their emergency plan, they picked up the victims and carried them to the friary where a hospital was set up. All during this first attack, Father Kolbe remained calm, keeping this situation under control as much as possible.

The next attack came on September 7 on Teresin, activating the air raid sirens. As some bombs landed on the monastery's reception area, friars yelled, "Father, take cover, take cover!" as Father Kolbe ran between buildings to check on the safety of the brothers and to comfort them. Only a new door was damaged, and no friars were injured.

Chapter 11

The First Arrests

On September 12, the friars of Niepokalanow and nearby residents of Paprotnia watched nervously as the Polish army retreated toward Warsaw after being overrun by the powerful Nazi army. Anxiety was high because everyone fearfully awaited the arrival of the Germans. The friars didn't know if the Germans would attack the monastery and kill everyone there or simply ignore them as Brother Juventyn noted in his journal:

> In Niepokalonow, as for all people in Poland, these were the days of suffering and terror The shock experienced by the defeat on the battlefront, the prospect of the loss of freedom, the bombardment, and the uncertainty of what the invaders would—all this was a terrible psychological trial for everyone. . . . Every day during our morning meditation, Father Maximilian reminded us that this might be the last day of our life and tried to prepare us for a happy death.

With the sound of the monastery bells ringing at 10:00 AM as normal on September 19, 1939, there was a knock at the front door. Opening the door, Father Kolbe found himself, not surprisingly, facing a Wehrmacht (German army) officer who announced, "Until the situation in Poland is stabilized, the monastery is to be closed." Father Kolbe asked to be allowed to keep the infirmary open since they were attending to several citizens who had been critically wounded during a recent attack and attempts to move them could result in their death. Not expecting this petition, the officer pondered it and then told Father Kolbe that two friars could remain to operate the infirmary. All others, including Father Kolbe, had to leave, eventually being sent to internment camps.

Father Kolbe assembled the brothers and relayed the officer's orders. The disappointed friars insisted that their leader stay and care for the monastery as well as for himself because he was in frail health. Kolbe was aware of their concern for him, but he knew he knew he had to obey the German officer. He likely felt fortunate that at least two friars could take care of the injured. He appointed Brother Witold Garlo to be in charge of the infirmary and Brother Cyriak Szubionmski to be his assistant.

The brothers gathered in groups of five and left, headed for a future known only to their Savior. As the last ones walked out of the door, the German soldiers sat down at the dining table and enjoyed the pancakes and wild berries that had been prepared for the friars. Meanwhile the friars marched about three-quarters of a mile to the Posnan-Warsaw highway, where buses were awaiting them. Along the way, on both sides of the road, citizens of Paprotnia who had been instrumental in building Niepokalanow stood tearfully, praying for their friends, not knowing whether they would ever return. At the end of the day, forty-eight friars, including several visiting friars, were sent to Germany.

When the friars reached their destination, they were immediately instructed to unload artillery shells from trucks and deposit them in a nearby field. During this task, one of the guards noticed that Father Kolbe was using a cane. The soldier shouted, "What! A prisoner with a cane?" He snatched the cane and threw it into the field. Keenly aware of the likely outcome of trying to retrieve the cane, Kolbe continued on with his work as if nothing happened. Fortunately, his cane was returned to him that evening by a kinder officer.

After completing their work assignment, the friars were herded onto trucks—like cows being taken to the slaughter house—for a forty-mile journey to the town of Rawa Mazowiecka. As the friars boarded the trucks, Father Maximilian reminded them that they were on a mission of converting souls and how fortunate they were that the Germans were providing all of their transportation without costing their order one cent!

After an hour or so, the drivers pulled up to the Passionist Fathers' Church of the Assumption, which had been commandeered by the Germans. As the friars walked through the doors of the sanctuary, they were met by other prisoners of war, who, like them, were weary and hungry from a long and stressful day.

Once everyone was settled they were informed that they would receive no food until the next day, a message that made a bad day even worse. The only thing to do was to try to regain some strength by sleeping and hope to have breakfast when they awoke.

When morning arrived, a large group of local Rawa Mazowiecka residents were gathered in the town square demanding that the German soldiers allow them to serve food they had prepared for those housed in the sanctuary. Finally, after some deliberation, the captors permitted the crowd to feed the starving prisoners. After breakfast the prisoners were ordered to file out and board the trucks for a ninety-mile journey to the city of Czestachowa.

As the convoy approached Czestachowa, crowds of sympathizers lined the road throwing food to the captives and loudly encouraging them to jump from the trucks and flee their captors. Some offered civilian clothing in the event that the friars were successful. While some captives likely gave serious thought to escaping, they realized there was little chance of success. The drivers hurried on and stopped at a railroad station. There the prisoners were loaded onto freight cars often used for transporting animals and then continued on to their ultimate destination somewhere in Nazi occupied Germany.

Father Kolbe could read the hearts and minds of his fellow friars and knew they were filled with apprehension for their lives and their futures. As a gifted spiritual leader and motivator, he encouraged them during this turbulent time. Once they got underway, he said, "Remember, dear children, that the prayers and witness of Paul and Silas in the Philippian jail led not only to their liberation but also to the conversion of their jailer and his family and began the dissemination of the Gospel in Europe. Remember also that later, even during his house arrest in Rome before his martyrdom, Paul did not cease to proclaim the Gospel to everyone in his environment, including members of Caesar's household, who, as rulers of the world, heard from the lips of the great apostle the Gospel of the world's redeemer."

The train crossed over into Germany and stopped at Lamsdorf (present-day Lambinowice). Everyone disembarked and was placed into one truck. More prisoners were added to this group, including Polish Jews, soldiers, and Ukrainians, making a total of six hundred. After traveling for many hours, the prisoners were extremely thirsty and at each station where they stopped they desperately pleaded for water, especially for an ill prisoner. The guards refused to allow the German workers to give them water. One said in an arrogant voice, "Don't give them any water, the Polish swine."

When they arrived at Legnica, one of the priests aboard begged a German soldier for water. The soldier filled a bottle with water and tried to pass it to the priest through a small window in the boxcar. As he did so, another soldier knocked the bottle out of his hand and said, "They're all destined for extermination." Finally, at one stop, the station master was able to allow the prisoners to disembark, get water for them, and provide them with tea and cookies, a stark but much welcomed treat.

After a journey of more than two hundred miles, the train pulled into Amtitz (now Gebice), a village in West Central Poland where prisoners were placed in an internment camp. The camp's capacity was twelve thousand prisoners, two hundred in each tent. A barbed wire fence around the perimeter and towers manned by heavily armed guards ensured that no prisoner escaped. The tents were extremely uncomfortable. They leaked in rainy weather, and because the beds were straw on bare ground, they absorbed the water. Each tent had two long wood dining tables and two benches constructed of rough timber. Food was scant. Breakfast was unsweetened ersatz coffee or soup; the noon meal consisted of a half quart of soup along with small pieces of carrots, turnips, potatoes, or cabbage; the evening meal was also ersatz coffee and soup. The soup was made from sifted flour and water. Meat and fat were never included in a meal. Although the internment camp meals were the same as in the concentration camps, the advantage was not having to perform hard labor as required in the concentration camps.

Naturally, Father Maximilian and the other friars felt the effects of the trauma they had been subjected to on the journey. Once in the barracks, they were able to continue a daily routine similar to what it was in Niepokolanow. One brother was able to mold a statue of the Blessed Mother out of clay as he had done formerly. The friars managed to do some evangelizing. They made friends with Sergeant Sturn, the officer in charge of their tent. Sturn was a Protestant from Berlin and chose Brother Telesfor Bobrycki, who spoke fluent German, to be his translator. This brother introduced Sergeant Sturn to Father Kolbe, which led to many friendly conversations, including discussions about their Christian faith. Later, Sturn introduced Father Kolbe to Lieutenant Zalewski, who was of Polish ancestry. Through their common heritage, the two men developed a close relationship, and Kolbe was able to learn what was happening in the war outside the camp.

In the meantime, hostile guards assigned to Father Kolbe's tent provoked the prisoners by showing pictures of the war's destruction of Polish cities and placing blame on England. With tears in his eyes, Father Maximilian commented to his friars, "Poland will be resurrected and this very ground on which we now stand, our prison, one day will be inside a united and independent Poland."

Shortly after arriving in Amtitz, the prisoners received the distressing news that Warsaw had capitulated to the German army, overtaken by their bombers, tanks, and artillery. Father Kolbe gave solace to his friars, saying in part, "Great nations will fall, but only an unworthy nation can perish."

On October 6, the German government made a major announcement regarding the partitioning of Poland. Germany would incorporate a large part of western Poland, while Stalin would be compensated for his August 23 treaty by being given a large area of eastern Poland along with a free hand in the Baltic states. The remaining portions of Poland would be under German rule. In the same announcement, it was reported that 10,572 German soldiers had died during the war with Poland.

On Monday November 6, Father Kolbe was visited by Lieutenant Zalewski and Sergeant Sturn, who brought some welcome news. They informed him that, perhaps as early as the next day, the friars would be released and transported to a different location, although the two soldiers didn't know where. The next day, just as the guards had said, Father Kolbe and his friars left Amtitz on a train. Their hope was to arrive at the train station in Szymanow next to the Niepokalaow friary. They were disappointed when, after a 183-mile journey, they were directed to get off the train at Schildberg in west central Poland (now Ostrzeszow). Although they were frustrated, at least they were much closer to the friary and gave thanks to God for this favor granted to them.

They lined up as expected and were ordered to jog to their new detention facility, which, oddly enough, was a gymnasium at a secondary school previously used by the Salesian Fathers but commandeered by the Germans for a new internment camp.

Once the friars arrived, they were directed to the basement, where they were instructed to remove the old straw on the floor, which had been contaminated with lice, and replace it with new straw. Father Maximilian, always looking for some good in a bad situation, commented, "At least the basement is dry, and we have stone walls to protect us from the dampness."

As word got around town that the Franciscans from Niepokalanow were in the school, the local community began to gather food. They brought it to the friars, who were delighted and thankful to receive it. Through the direction of the Sisters of

Charles Borromeo, assistance was also rendered by the Polish Red Cross, who arranged medical examinations for the friars and dispensed necessary medication.

On November 17, a new commandant, Lieutenant Hans Mulzer, took over the reins of the Schildberg internment center and immediately initiated some positive changes. First, he met with Brother Hieronim, a German interpreter, who asked about getting more food for the friars because some were experiencing medical problems caused by insufficient vitamins in the food served in their former camp. Furthermore, he asked if he could go to the city and beg for food and medicine, believing that Polish townspeople would willingly provide it for the Polish friars. Lieutenant Mulzer asked Brother Hieronim to have Father Kolbe meet with him to see what arrangements they might make. During the meeting, the commandant made an offer that Father Kolbe could not resist. He explained that the citizens who were operating the kitchen at the center were giving some food to friends, causing a food shortage for the prisoners. Acutely aware of the Franciscans' honesty, he proposed allowing them to beg for food if they would take over the operation of the kitchen. This was a win-win offer. Without hesitation, Father Maximilian gratefully accepted it.

The Franciscans organized a network of volunteers to collect donated items and deliver them to Dr. Szustak, who had agreed to use his office for temporary storage. From there Brother Cyprian Grodzki and other volunteers transported the donations to the school. Knowing that Lieutenant Mulzer was a Lutheran minister and because this officer had been so accommodating, Father Kolbe asked his permission to take the inmates to the local church and say Mass. Commandant Mulzer, however, declined, citing his concern for his own welfare and that of the friars. He did agree, though, to invite one of the local priests to bring Holy Communion to the school. With great appreciation for this unexpected counter offer, Father Maximilian promised to pray for the commandant.

More good news came when the commandant announced that the Franciscans were to be released the next day, December 8, 1939. Not only was this the Feast of the Immaculate Conception, but the twelfth anniversary of the consecration of the friary at Niepokalanow. Father Kolbe and the Militia Immaculatae saw this as a sign and a special grace coming through the prayers of the Blessed Mother.

On December 8, Father Thomasz Sworski, a local priest, brought Holy Communion, something the prisoners had not had the benefit of in quite some time. Father Kolbe recognized this as another sign of divine grace courtesy of the Blessed Mother.

Before being released, Father asked if a photograph could be taken of the friars with Lieutenant Mulzer. He also wanted to present the Protestant minister with a miraculous medal. Both actions were in violation of the strict internment camp regulations and could result in grave consequences. However, since Lieutenant Mulzer had already broken one of the other rules, he allowed the photo and accepted the gift of the medal. He said, "I hope one day to visit your friary." The photograph is now on display at the Kolbe museum in Niepokalanow.

After lunch, Lieutenant Mulzer gave Father Maximilian a one-half pound of butter as a parting gift and said he was sorry he did not have more to give him. He asked that the friars share the butter with other prisoners, something they would have done instinctively anyway. So the friars gave small pieces of bread and some butter to a few other prisoners being released that day. Despite the Nazis' best efforts to pit Germans against the Polish through vitriolic propaganda, the Protestant minister and the Franciscan priest left each other with "deep mutual respect, their commitment to the Gospel of Christ enabling them to transcend the environment of hate."

As the friars walked to the train station, looking forward to returning to Niepokalanow, they joyfully sang patriotic Polish songs. Gathered along the streets were citizens of Schildberg, waving to their much-loved friars as they passed by. A number of women ran up to them, handing out sacks of freshly made bread.

Reaching the train station shortly before their 4:00 PM departure for the 175-mile journey to Warsaw, the prisoners immediately boarded the trains. Unlike their previous rail cars used for transporting cattle, these trains were equipped with wooden benches. Although the prisoners were not sitting on cushioned seats, these trains were an upgrade for which they were thankful.

On the way, several brothers were concerned for Father Kolbe's safety because he was the head of the friary and the chief editor and publisher of *Rycerz Niepokalanej*, which was critical of the Nazis. They suggested that he hide from the Gestapo, the German secret police. Father Kolbe explained that he was the shepherd of his flock and therefore could not abandon them. He felt a moral obligation to defend the place that he, his brother friars, and neighbors had worked so hard to build. The brothers no longer brought up the matter.

On December 9 at 7:00 AM, the friars detrained in Warsaw and saw people walking around in psychological ruins from their defeat, their heads hanging low. More depressing was the sight of the anguished faces of Jews wearing Nazi issued shirts with the star of David displayed on the sleeves to mark them as Jewish.

The group went to a Franciscan monastery on Zakroczymska Street and visited awhile. Then four priests and forty brothers left for the final leg of the trip to Niepokalanow. Father Maximilian, however, remained to take care of business with the Provincial and then left the following day.

Chapter 12

Back at Niepokalanow

Arriving at Niepokalanow on December 10, 1939, Father Kolbe was saddened to see the destruction there, although the buildings were for the most part still habitable. The friars began the task of surveying the damage and noted that much had been stolen, including the kitchenware and an assortment of hand tools, presumably now in possession of the Nazis. Initially they were pleased to see that the presses were still there, but, regrettably, the Germans had sealed them, putting a stop to future publications. In the main buildings, it was apparent that the civilian administrators of the Wehrmacht and German government had set up offices there.

Given the unsettled situation, Father Kolbe knew beyond doubt that things would only get worse. It was expected that the enemies, who were nearby, would return and arrest him because he was one of the intellectuals and a Catholic priest. Along with him they would arrest all the friars. The only question was when. Yes, things were going to be different, but the ever-optimistic Father Kolbe would find a way to establish some form of normalcy, not knowing how much time he or the others had.

Among the first priorities Father Kolbe identified was to restore the chapel for daily Mass and adoration. After all, wasn't paying homage to God the only way to start each day?

Over the next couple of days, the friars established a refugee center. Refugees from nearby Paprotnia confessed to Father Kolbe that they were the ones who had taken the kitchenware and tools. They explained, "We thought the monastery was to be abandoned. We reasoned if no one is to live here, why should the Germans benefit from what the Franciscans had to leave behind." This small ray of sunshine in an otherwise bleak time surely brought smiles to the Franciscans' faces.

In the end, the Franciscans housed some 3,500 refugees, which included 1,500 Jews, from the Poznam area. Stories about the hostility and abuses that occurred at the behest of the Poznam District Governor Arthur Greiser and his deputy Jaeger were related. The refugees warned the Franciscans of what Greiser said: "In my Gau region the church no longer is a problem. Because they are nationalists, we place the Polish priests in secure arrest, and the Protestant clergy we conscript and send them to die for Fuhrer and Fatherland."

Besides the refugee center, a hospital, a machinery repair shop, and a dairy were created as the friars adapted their buildings to their new mission. Father Kolbe formulated a new mission statement:

> We must do everything in our power to aid these unfortunate countrymen ripped from the bosom of their families and without livelihood. Our mission now is, in the name of Immaculata, to work for the benefit of these souls. Our immediate challenge is to care for our expatriated countrymen expelled from those regions of Poland now incorporated in the Third Reich. We must house them, feed them, and provide for their spiritual and physical needs. There is to be no distinction made because of religious or ethnic identity. They are all Poles.

An excellent administrator, Father Kolbe set up an organizational structure, a self-government that integrated the refugee population with the friars. He also arranged for a stable supply of food by choosing brothers and refugees to go into neighborhoods and beg. This worked quite well for the time being, but his long-term plan was setting up a farm on the property with livestock and vegetable gardens in order to be more self-sustaining. He asked all residents to be involved in work to support the group, depending on their qualifications. This included farm work; health care; repairing machinery, bicycles, watches, and so forth; and various other undertakings. Fortunately, some residents were doctors and could care for the refugees' health. Father Kolbe's goal was to make Niepokalanow such an invaluable facility that the National Socialist Party would want the residents to remain. Ultimately, the priest's stratagem failed but did bring some peace and stability in the interim.

Father Kolbe also petitioned authorities to allow those friars who had been displaced previously to return to Niepokalanow so they could use their skills to assist the refugees. Surprisingly, he received permission, and many of them did return and provided valuable services.

High on Father Kolbe's agenda, as soon as he had things calmed down, was to restart printing *Rycerz Niepokalanej.* He made two trips to Sochaczew to gain permission, but both times the officials he needed to speak to were not there. He then wrote a letter requesting authorization, but the response was not to his satisfaction: he could resume publishing, but the presses would not be unsealed. Father Kolbe returned to Sochaczew hoping that appealing in person would carry more weight. However, because he had published some unfavorable cartoons of Hitler, he was denied permission to use the presses. Discouraged but undefeated, Father Kolbe would find another avenue to keep the presses running.

On Christmas Eve, 1939, despite the circumstances the friars were living with, they were filled with happiness as preparations were underway for celebrating the birth of Jesus Christ. They shared their meal with the new residents and distributed cookies to the many children. The friars and others celebrated Midnight Mass with much joy.

Since the invasion, the city was flooded with Jews, and Father Kolbe in Christian charity welcomed them to the friary with open arms. During the Christmas season Father Kolbe had a Christmas party for all Christian residents, but he also held a new year's celebration for all those of the Jewish faith. Despite their religious differences, Christians and Jews lived very well together although the media often reported an opposite story.

The Franciscan brothers were now taking care of hundreds of refugees on a daily basis. Each day the infirmary was seeing between sixty to seventy people ranging from the very young to the very old. The pharmacy was dispensing about twenty prescriptions a day, and the hospital in the dining room accommodated thirty patients, mostly refugees. The machine and carpentry shops were working at maximum capacity and had to turn down additional work because only one-fourth of the friars remained. Coming into the machine shop for repair were harvesters, planting machines, motorcycles, bicycles, and winches. The carpentry shop was busy making tables, chairs, and benches for the refugee population as well as for the friary in Sochaczew. Friars supervised the preparation of meals for the 1,500 refugees, and bakers made sure there was an adequate supply of daily bread. Other brothers were assigned to take of the residents' additional needs.

Father Maximilian did not limit his work to the friary but extended it to the neighbors who had helped the friars in the past, even though the Franciscans risked the threat of bullets and bombs. For example, since the friary had the luxury of electrical generators, Father Kolbe directed the friars to extend electrical lines to the train station.

As the war escalated, several small bombs landed on the monastery. They caused major damage to the central part of the reception area, but, by the grace of God, no injuries were sustained. There was growing concern each day as to when and where the next bomb might hit and what injuries and deaths might occur.

As February 1940 drew to a close, the friary refugees were slated to be transferred to other locations. Before departing, a Jewish woman approached Brother Lukasz Kuzba, who had taken care of the Jewish residents' needs and said, "We wish to present an expression of our collective gratitude to the Guardian of

Niepokalanow. From the Franciscans here, we have received loving and sympathetic care. Here in Niepokalanow we have been surrounded by kindness for which we now, in the name of all Jewish inhabitants, wish to render sincere thanks to Father Maximilian and to his friars. Therefore, we request that a Holy Mass of thanksgiving be celebrated to thank God for protection over us and over Niepokalanow." With that she handed him a large monetary donation. Then another Jewish resident, Shimon Levy, said to Brother Lukasz, "If God permits us to survive this war, we'll repay Niepokalanow a hundredfold. The hospitality demonstrated to our Poznan Jewish community we'll never forget. We'll praise it everywhere and make certain others don't forget."

No sooner had these refugees left, when a second group arrived, who were exiled from Pomerania, an area on the southern shore of the Baltic Sea and split between Germany and Poland. Through one of them, a lawyer named Stanislaw Kozinski, Father Kolbe learned of atrocities being inflicted on the Polish citizens. Kozinski said, "Father, the Germans are divided in their occupational policy towards us. We've heard, for example, that Wehrmaht officers have complained to their superiors concerning the actions of the SS special units. It's the SS special units, which are not under the command of the Wehrmacht officers, which perpetrate the brutalities." Father Kolbe responded, "Yes, we've heard of SS special units. Fortunately, the German garrison stationed at Niepokalanow is made of Wehrmacht and not the SS."

One day particularly hard for Father Kolbe was April 20, 1940, because it was Adolph Hitler's fifty-first birthday and to commemorate this event, German officials draped a large swastika flag over the entrance of the main building at Niepokalanow. Adjacent to this flag was a banner with these words in large black letters: *Ein Reich, Ein Volk, Ein Fuhrer* (One Empire, One Nation, One Leader). This prominent display was a violation of the buildings dedicated to the promotion of Christianity. Father Kolbe told his brothers, "It appears for the present that evil has triumphed, but we know that God still reigns and that Our Lady will not permit us to be tempted beyond what we're able to bear. Pray with me, children, that God will hasten the day when this hated symbol will no longer deface the buildings dedicated to the Immaculata. Hitlerism ultimately is doomed."

The mission of the friars at Niepokalanow gained momentum even though it was well known that the friars opposed the Third Reich. Many friars were returning to help care for the refugees despite the dangers. Although many other monasteries had been closed, Niepokalanow thrived, offering community services, such as its fire brigade. New life had been breathed into what could have been deserted land and buildings.

On May 30, 1940, Hitler's personal attorney, Hans Frank, penned in his diary words that gave credence to the dangers facing the Franciscans:

> The Fuhrer informed me that those persons identified as leaders in the Polish nation are to be liquidated. We also are to mark those who might become future leaders and at the appropriate time liquidate them. The clergy are to preach what we command them to preach. If they act against this prescription, they are to receive short shrift.

October 12, 1940, was Father Kolbe's name day, for it was the feast of St. Maximilius, his patron saint. On this occasion he wrote the following to his fellow brothers:

> The occupation of our nation intensifies our patriotism. I often have thought about our struggle for independence in 1914. If I had been in Poland, I probably would have joined my brother Waleryan in enlisting in the legionaries. I doubt if I could have restrained myself from responding to my country's call for her sons to rise up and liberate our people.
>
> God works in mysterious ways. By sending me to Rome in 1912, the Immaculata demonstrated to me that

> her will was not that I should become a legionnaire to fight with carnal weapons for the independence of her nation. The Immaculata enlisted me in a cosmopolitan crusade to fight with her spiritual weapons for her universal sovereignty.
>
> You, my children, have joined me in this campaign. We love our nation and are ardent patriots, but we must first serve God and His Holy Mother in the ranks of the Militia Immaculatae. If we perform our duty to Poland's queen and our Immaculata, she certainly will rescue and restore our nation.

Father Kolbe still prayed about publishing *The Knight* and continued to nudge the Nazis to allow him to print another edition. Finally his attitude and reasoning persuaded Dr. Grundmann, the director of the Warsaw District Board of Public Education and Propaganda, to have a permit issued. Two and a half weeks before the Feast of the Immaculate Conception, a letter arrived with the written permit, but only one edition was allowed. It would be limited to 120,000 copies and restricted to Warsaw.

As Father Isidore Kozbial, the editor, was preparing the issue, Father Maximilian told him, "It isn't important whether *The Knight* gets out, but it is important that the endeavor be surrounded by prayers—and be sent out accompanied by prayers."

Knowing that for at least the foreseeable future he would not be able to publish communications about Niepokalanow, the messages of the Immaculata, and the Gospels, Father Kolbe wrote the following as a final article of the edition to serve as part of his legacy: "No one in the world can alter the truth. All that we can do is seek it, find it, and live it. . . . If good consists in the love of God and springs from love, evil is substantially a negation of love." This last issue of *The Knight* was published on December 8. To avoid Nazis' intercepting copies at the post office, they were delivered personally to the priests and residents. Afterward, numerous letters from readers arrived expressing their joy at receiving *The Knight* and bearing comments like, "The dawn of liberty arises." The friars knelt and offered prayers of thanksgiving to their patroness, the Immaculata.

The Nazis regretted having given permission for Father Kolbe to print this last edition because it exposed the evils of the Nazi ideology to its readers and thus to the world. Because the Kolbe name was German, they tried to convert him to their way of thinking. Not surprisingly, their words fell on deaf ears and he vigorously defended his Polish nationality.

This year's Christmas would be the final one for Father Kolbe and many of the Franciscan friars. He knew that the war would be the path that would take him to Christ, the Immaculata, and the saints. Being in the company of his brothers and the refugees had special meaning for him, and he cherished the opportunity to share this last Christmas with them.

Before Mass began, Brother Iwo introduced Father Kolbe to Corporal Holzer, a twenty-six-year-old Wehrmacht officer assigned to the friary. He was a Catholic and wished to attend Mass and receive the Eucharist with the residents. Maximilian greeted him with a smile and a handshake, saying, "All who love our Lord Jesus and his holy mother are welcome to worship with us." This was a surreal moment—a conquering German asking a favor from one of the conquered. No doubt, this exceptional Christmas gift pleased Father Kolbe and united the two men in an extraordinary way.

On January 8, 1941, Father Maximilian celebrated his forty-seventh birthday. Addressing his friars, he reflected on his decision to become a friar and all of the events of his journey. He also thanked all of them for the birthday salutations and their dedication to their duties as friars. Then he said, "Children, I'll not survive the war. Many of you will survive, and it's left to you to carry on the work we've begun together." Needless to say, his friars were greatly saddened by these remarks and hoped and prayed that he was wrong. But deep in their hearts, they knew that the situation was quite grim and that his prediction could be trusted because he was a great mystic. He was like Jesus preparing the disciples for his passion: “From that time on, Jesus began to show his disciples that he must go to Jerusalem and undergo great suffering at the hands of the elders and chief priest and scribes, and be killed, and on the third day be raised” (Matthew 16:21–22).

Chapter 13

Final Farewell to Niepokalanow

Brother Arnold Wedrowski was sitting at his typewriter one morning in February of 1941, recording thoughts about the relations between Trinity and Immaculate Conception that Father Maximilian dictated in preparation for a book he planned to write. While Father Kolbe usually only wore his best habit on Sundays and feast days, he elected to wear it this weekday. Perhaps he had a premonition of things to come, or maybe someone let him know that the Gestapo would arrive that morning.

After the first part of the dictation, Father Maximilian dropped to his knees and said the Hail Mary three times. About 9:50 AM, Brother Ivo, who was responsible for receiving visitors, observed two cars with Gestapo license plates driving up to the reception center. He called Father Kolbe and said, "Father, two automobiles marked POL [police] just entered the friary compound. There are five uniformed men and one man in civilian clothes." Father Kolbe said, "Oh? All right, all right, my child. Maria." Looking at the statue of the Virgin Mary, he mused, "It was twenty-four years ago on this date on St. Peter's Square when the enemies of faith launched their vehement assault against our Church and against our Holy Father. Now new enemies seek to destroy our Church and our nation. Since the outbreak of hostilities, we have known that, sooner or later, Niepokolanow, as a center of Polish Catholicism and patriotism, would come under attack."

Father Kolbe proceeded to the reception area where he encountered the Security Police. The man in civilian clothes identified himself as the agent-in-charge and asked for a tour of the friary. Father Kolbe obliged, accompanied by two of the Gestapo officers. They toured the buildings for two hours. On returning to the reception area, Father Maximilian offered the guests some tea; however the agent replied, "Priest, you don't seem to understand.

We're here not to drink your tea but to place you and four of your priests under arrest." These priests were also involved in publishing *The Knight*. Putting up no defense, Father Kolbe called for Father Justyn Nazim, Father Pius Bartosik, Father Urban Cieslak, and Father Antonion Bajewski; and they were all walked to the police car. Brother Pelagiusz quickly went to the kitchen to get bread for their journey.

As Father Kolbe was about to get into the police car, which resembled a hearse, he turned to the brothers who had gathered and were standing there shocked and silent. He blessed them and Niepokalanow with the Sign of the Cross, knowing that this was the last time on earth he would see his beloved friars and the City of Immaculata he founded. Then Father Kolbe entered the car, and the friars saw him turn his face and look out the rear window as the police car left. Ironically, the following day, in Krakow, 200 miles from Niepokalanow, an elderly man named Karol Josef Wojtyla, Sr., died, leaving only one son, twenty-year-old Karol Josef Wojtyla, Jr., who would become Pope John Paul II and canonize Father Maximilian Kolbe.

Father Kolbe and his fellow priests were en route to the notorious Piawak prison situated on the edge of the Jewish ghetto in Warsaw. The prison opened in 1835 and was named after the street on which it was built. Now it was under the control of the Gestapo, and from 1940 until the end of the war an estimated 37,000 people died there in secret or through public executions.

When Father Kolbe was being checked in by prison officials in Piawak, they remarked on his name and suggest that he could easily pass for German, which would possibly alter his fate. True to his Polish nationality and repulsed by the thought of such a thing, he adamantly refused the offer. He wished to carry any cross that would come his way. Consequently, he was placed in block 6, cell 103 with the other nineteen prisoners, waiting each day and not knowing where they would be going.

Wasting no time or talents, Father Kolbe began ministering to the other prisoners. One of the SS officers noticed his Franciscan habit with the rosary and cross attached to the cord around his waist. Angrily, the officer yanked off the rosary and shouted to the priest, "Do you believe in this?" Father Kolbe answered calmly, "Yes, I believe." Enraged, the German struck Father Kolbe in the face, drawing blood. Three times the officer repeated the question and, receiving the same answer, struck the priest, who remained calm. After the officer left, Father Kolbe walked up and down in the cell, praying. He soothed the other prisoners, saying, "There is no reason for getting upset. . . This is a small thing; everything for the Immaculata."

During the time of Father Kolbe's confinement, his fellow brothers outside of the camp made a concerted effort to seek his release. They even brought a petition to the chief of the security police with a list of twenty friars who were willing to be hostages in his place. In response, the chief wrote: "A noble gesture, however the Guardian of your cloister is more important to us than all of the Franciscans living there. We have your leaders. There is only one way we can keep this nation subjugated, and that's to deprive the Polish people of their spiritual and intellectual leadership. In your Father Kolbe we have both a spiritual and intellectual leader."

Father Kolbe, ever diligent in performing his priestly duties, smuggled into the camp consecrated Communion wafers with the help of Polish guards. Tragically, after an investigation, forty-five guards were found guilty of this violation of prison security regulations and sent to concentration camps. Ten of them were executed. Their jobs as security detail were turned over to SS and non-Polish officers.

The poor conditions in the camp led to Father Kolbe contracting pneumonia. While he was recovering in the prison infirmary, on April 4 the four priests who accompanied him to Pawiak prison were transferred to the Auschwitz concentration camp. Two of them died there: Father Bajewski on May 8, 1941, and Father Bartosik on December 13. Both priests were beatified on June 13, 1999, along with 108 victims of the Nazi atrocities.

The other two priests were transferred to Dachau on May 3, 1941, where they were eventually released. While engaged in missionary work in Japan, Father Cieslak passed away on November 11, 1960. After serving as chaplain in Rockford, Illinois, Father Nazim served in Japan for fourteen years and died on December 31, 1966.

After recuperating, Father Kolbe worked at the Pawiak prison library and heard prisoners' confessions. He communicated with the friars at Niepokalanow, although all incoming and outgoing mail was limited and scrutinized by prison officials. Postcards could be sent with requests for certain provisions such as food and clothing. Parcels of food could be received only twice a month and weigh no more than eleven pounds. Nothing about the living conditions at Pawiak could be mentioned in correspondence.

Chapter 14

Auschwitz

> We who lived in concentration camps can remember the men who walked through the huts comforting others, giving away their last piece of bread. They may have been few in number, but they offer sufficient proof that everything can be taken from a man but one thing: the last of the human freedoms—to choose one's attitude—in any given circumstances, to choose one's own way.
>
> ~ Viktor E. Frankl, *Man's Search for Meaning*

On Wednesday, May 28, 1941, prison guards took Father Kolbe, along with 304 other prisoners, to a train station, packed them into cattle cars, and transferred them to the Auschwitz concentration camp. During the journey, they were given nothing to eat or drink and their toilet was a bucket. The stench from the straw, which was laden with human excrement, was almost unbearable. Grown men wept like children in their agony and fear. Most saw their destination as the place where they would die. What the huddled masses were presently experiencing was just a preview of what awaited them in Auschwitz. No doubt, some wished to die on the train. It would be a better alternative than the living conditions they were about to experience.

To lift the spirits of the downtrodden prisoners, Father Kolbe with his constant love for people began to sing religious and patriotic songs and encouraged others to do so. Many joined in to fend off their discouragement and depression.

The Polish town of Oswiecim (Auschwitz in German) was strategically located in southern Poland near the fork of the Sola and Vistula Rivers. It was chosen for the housing and extermination of political prisoners because its central location in Nazi territories protected it from invaders. Moreover, there were railroads close by, making it easy to transport large numbers of prisoners quickly. Demographics of the area were advantageous as well. Not many people lived in the swampy and unhealthy area. SS officers confronted them and ordered them to leave the area or risk being shot without warning if they trespassed. Many left, while others remained there because they had no other place to go.

After the prisoners were unloaded from the train, SS officers marched them past vicious police dogs who lunged at them, deterring anyone who thought of escaping. Further along the way, the prisoners were subjected to flogging. As they walked through the gate of the notorious concentration camp, they could look up at the iron archway and see the words *Arbeit Macht Frei* (Work makes you free). Although this suggested that if one worked hard it was possible to be freed, it is doubtful that any prisoner believed this and was consoled. On the contrary, the prisoners probably were more inclined to recall Dante's *Divine Comedy* in which the gate of hell bears the words "Abandon all hope, ye who enter here." (comparison from Claude R. Foster, *Mary's Knight*, p. 700.)

Once inside the camp, Father Kolbe and the other prisoners were stripped of their clothing, sent to the showers, sprayed with a disinfectant, and shaved of all body hair. Next they were handed their uniform of vertical blue and gray stripes, often stained with blood from the previous owner. One the left side of the shirt was a cloth badge: an inverted triangle whose color identified the reason the prisoner was there. Father Kolbe's triangle was red, designating him as a political prisoner, and in the center was the letter *P* for Pole. Below the triangle was his identification number: 16670.

After being outfitted with uniforms, the prisoners assembled in rows. Deputy Commandant Karl Fritch, who was in charge of Father Kolbe's bunker, addressed them. He told the prisoners that they were not at a sanatorium but in a concentration camp and there was only one exit, through the chimney of the crematorium. However, they might choose to leave by trying to climb the electrified fence. Fritch added that those who were

Jewish could expect to live in the camp for two weeks, priests for one month, and the rest for three months. When his speech was concluded, the prisoners were led to their bunker, wondering what would happen next.

During the time of Father Maximilian's confinement, the camp was run by Rudolf Hess, a German born in 1900 to Francis Xavier and Lina Hess. Raised in a devout family, he served as an altar boy and, hoping that he would become a priest, his family took him on pilgrimages to Lourdes and Einsiedeln, a Swiss municipality known for its Benedictine Abbey. However, after losing his parents by the time he was seventeen, Hess fought in World War I, became a member of the National Socialism movement, and enlisted in the German army. Later on, he renounced his Catholic faith and joined the Nazi Party. There is no recorded evidence that Father Kolbe ever met with Hess. One can speculate what might have transpired if the priest had had the opportunity to dialogue with him before he abandoned the faith.

A few days after Father Kolbe and his companions arrived, Commandant Fritsch entered their block and ordered all of the priests to step forward. He said, "Follow me," and led them to an ex-con by the name of Krott nicknamed Bloody Krott because of his brutality. Krott was the taskmaster of the commando at Babice. Fritsch said, "Krott, teach each of these miserable parasites what work is." Krott replied, "Leave it to me, Herr Commandant."

Among other jobs, Krott was to take prisoners to a forest, have them place large tree limbs on their shoulders, and run to a field where they dropped them. Krott had Father Kolbe carry the heaviest limbs until he collapsed. After kicking him, Krott ordered guards to give the priest fifty lashes. Thinking the priest was dead, Krott kicked him into a ditch, threw tree branches over his body, and left.

When that workday was over, several inmates went to where Father Maximilian lay and, to their shock and surprise, discovered that he was miraculously still alive. They picked him up and carried him to the infirmary. Even though about two hundred prisoners were awaiting treatment, when Dr. Rudolf Diem, a Polish Protestant, saw the extent of Father Kolbe's injuries, he went to tend to him immediately. Father Kolbe said "It's all right, Doctor. I'll wait my turn." The doctor arranged for Father Kolbe to be reassigned to another cell block. Krott gloated that the priest couldn't handle heavy limbs.

Later, in a long conversation with Father Kolbe, Dr. Diem admitted that he had lost his faith in God and asked how the priest could persevere in faith in divine providence in a place like the camp. Father Kolbe responded that Satan is delighted to convince him that his faith is folly. After promising to pray for the doctor, Father Kolbe quoted Nicholas von Zinzendorf, a Protestant leader, who said, "When life is difficult, stand firm and bear all burdens, patient under discipline's rod. For through suffering and sorrow, our path leads most certainly to God."

As a witness at Father Kolbe's canonization inquest, Dr. Diem stated, "I can say with certainly that during my four years in Auschwitz, I never saw such a sublime example of God's love of one's neighbor." What sustained Father Kolbe during these excruciating times was a foundation of prayer and the offering of his sufferings to God for the other prisoners.

Father Maximilian continued daily manual labor and often came near the brink of collapsing from exhaustion. For example, on one occasion a fellow prisoner, Henryk Sienkiewikcz, offered to exchange wheelbarrows so that Father Kolbe would have a smaller one. Unfortunately, a capo (a prisoner charged with supervising work) observed this and became angry. He walked over to Sienkiewikcz and told him to sit in the wheelbarrow filled with gravel and told Father Kolbe to wheel it to the designated site. After dropping off the gravel, Kolbe had to sit in the wheelbarrow while Sienkiewikcz pushed it back. That evening both men collapsed on their bunks from complete exhaustion.

On Sunday, June 15, 1941, Father Kolbe wrote what would be his final letter. It was addressed to his mother, who most influenced him and nurtured his spiritual life.

My Dearest Mamusia,
At the end of May I was transported to the Auschwitz camp. I'm well. Dearest Mamusia. Because our dear God is everywhere and thinks of everyone with great love, don't be concerned about me or my health. Since I don't know how long I'll be here, for the time being it would be best not to write.

Kolbe Rajmund

On Sunday, June 22, 1941, Father Maximilian was sent to a quarantine bunker because of a recurring fever. A generous fellow inmate offered him the top bunk where the air was a bit more plentiful. In typical Kolbe style, he immediately and politely refused the offer and took the lower bunk. He explained that by doing so, he would be closer to the door and could bless the dead as they were being taken to the crematorium and give absolution to the dying. As they passed, he blessed them with the Sign of the Cross and prayed, "Holy Mary, mother of God, pray for us sinners, now and at the hour of our death. Grant them eternal rest, O Lord."

Soon Father Kolbe was transferred to block 12, which housed the disabled prisoners. After a modest recovery, he was sent to block 14, which was for inmates who worked on various outside projects. On July 29, 1941, several hundred inmates were sent to harvest crops in a nearby field. Over the course of that day, a Polish inmate named Zygmunt Pilawski, number 14156, who was a former truck driver from Zatory, managed to escape from his work group despite the armed guards and attack dogs. At the afternoon roll call when Pilawski did not respond, the SS guard assumed that he had escaped. This caused what the Germans called Nazi Sippenjutiz; because the escapee could not be penalized, ten inmates who were closest to him would be punished by death. Pilawski's fate is unknown. Some reports say that he was rearrested on July 31, 1942, and put to death, while others say he was found dead in a latrine.

After the roll call, all of the prisoners were ordered to return to their bunkers. That night, the inmates in Pilawski's bunker received no supper and were required to stand at attention until 9:00 PM. The men found it difficult to sleep as they wondered what the next day would bring if the missing prisoner did not return.

The following morning, commandant Fritsch, accompanied by SS officer Gerhard Palitzsch, who had taken roll call, stood in front of six hundred apprehensive inmates assembled outside. The commandant announced that the escaped inmate had not been found, and they would be required to remain at attention until he was captured or until further notice.

The prisoners, who had been given no food or water, stood there in the grueling heat of July, awaiting word on whether ten of them would be sentenced to death in the starvation bunker. Finally they were given a half-hour break and served a small portion of soup. As the hours wore on, some of the prisoners collapsed. When early evening arrived, Fritsch and Palitzsch returned. Fritsch announced that the escaped prisoner had not returned. The scared prisoners watched as Fritsch, baton in hand and Palitzsch by his side, walked up and down the rows of inmates, like a lion seeking out his prey. Finding his first victim, he ordered brusquely, "Three paces forward." The shivering inmate obeyed, whining incoherently and almost collapsing. Palitzsch wrote down his number on a pad. The selection process continued. The two officers walked among the quivering skeletons clad in their striped pajama-like prison garb. At times, Fritsch pointed his baton at an inmate merely to see the terrified expression on his face and then lowered the baton and moved on. Stopping in front of one inmate, Fritsch stared into his anguished eyes for a long time, and then began to move his baton toward him. Like a beaten dog, the prisoner whimpered. Fritsch barked, "Open your mouth!" The prisoner obeyed and after brief examination, Fritsch moved on without selecting the man.

The tenth inmate selected was a Franciszek (Francis) Gajowniczek, a Polish army sergeant. When told to step forward, he began to weep bitterly, saying, "My poor wife, my poor children who will take care of them?" Fritsch began to beat the man with his ox hide whip but failed to stop the man's outburst.

Witnessing this scene from the rear was Father Kolbe. Perhaps he recalled how the Blessed Mother had offered him the red crown of martyrdom and saw this as his opportunity to acquire it. He had a few moments to decide whether to save or give his life. He found himself walking forward to the crown.

As Father Kolbe broke through the ranks toward the ten prisoners selected for death, a surprised and angered Fritsch yelled, "Back in line!" Continuing forward, Father Kolbe said, "I must speak to the commandant." As he approached the two officers, Fritsch reached for his gun, although the priest was too weak to overpower anyone. Noticing the red triangle insignia with the letter *P*, designating Father Kolbe as a Polish Christian Political Enemy, Fritsch asked, "What does this Polish pig want?" In fluent German, Father Kolbe replied, "I would like to take the place of one of the inmates selected." He explained that he was a Catholic priest and had no dependents, while Gajowniszek had a wife and children. He also pointed out that he was old and not as fit as the selected man. Father Kolbe asked Fritsch to let him take his place.

No doubt, Fritsch was amazed. Why would any sane individual have a death wish while others were praying for their freedom? Obviously, Fritsch was unaware of Kolbe's thinking or his passion for becoming a martyr. After a brief silence, he granted Father Maximilian's request and ordered Gajowniszek to step back in line. The saved man stood still shaking and wondering why a Polish priest would take his place.

Brother Ladislaus, one of the assembled inmates, testified, "The ten victims walked in front of me and I saw that Father Kolbe was staggering under the weight of one of the others as he upheld this man who could not walk with his own strength."

Regrettably, Gajowniszek never had the opportunity to thank Kolbe for his courage and selflessness, for talking was not allowed. When Maximilian turned his head and looked briefly at Gajowniszek, the saved man could only thank him with his eyes. Later he recalled, "I was stunned and could hardly grasp what was going on. The immensity of it. I, the condemned, am to live and someone else willingly and voluntarily offers his life for me—a stranger. Is this some dream or reality?"

Chapter 15

Receiving the Red Crown

Reminiscent of Jesus going to his cross on Calvary, the ten selected prisoners walked to the starvation bunker and entered cell 18, an eight-by-eight-foot cement block room in a basement. The only light came from a small window at ground level, and the only thing in the cell was a bucket the men used to relieve themselves.

The guards ordered the ten prisoners to disrobe completely. As the guards left, the last one said to the ten men, "In a few days you'll all dry up like tulip bulbs." Then he walked out the door and locked it. While struggling with the fact of their impending death, the prisoners used what little strength they had left to sing hymns and pray, led by Father Kolbe. Prisoners held in adjacent cells imitated them to the wonderment of the guards. One guard reported, "This priest, knowing that they are all going to die, has them singing and praying. Usually the prisoners are cursing and screaming at us. He's transformed the death chamber into a chapel. He must be an idiot." "Or a saint," added another guard.

Every day, accompanied by an SS guard, Bruno Borgowiec (inmate number 1192 from Selesia, Poland) entered the cell to empty the bucket and carry out the corpses. He became the most reliable source of information regarding the final days of the prisoners there. He reported that when he went into the bunker, Father Kolbe would gaze directly at the guards, who would then order, "Keep your eyes down, don't look at us." Father Kolbe would frequently quote the Bible and sayings of martyrs to prepare the suffering inmates for their death.

Over the course of the first week, without any food, the prisoners deteriorated. Borgowiec testified that each morning when he went to the cell, the bucket was empty. He stated, "I believe that the inmates were drinking their own urine."

While Father Kolbe lay dying on the floor, he showed uncompromising love for his fellow prisoners. He cradled them as they confessed their sins in voices growing weaker and weaker. As each one died in his arms, he said the Hail Mary and then gently closed their eyes. Then Borgoewiec would come, place the corpse on a cart, and take it to the crematorium for incineration.

As Father Kolbe inched closer to his own death, he prayed for his brothers in Niepokolanow. He knew that they would perpetuate the organization he started so many years ago to convert others to Christ and his Blessed Mother.

After two weeks, four inmates were left in cell 18, and of them only Father Kolbe was fully conscious. The SS guards were impatient for them to die because space was needed for other prisoners. They asked Hans Bock, a physician at Auschwitz, to hasten their death. The doctor went to the cell with a needle filled with carbolic acid and began injecting each of the remaining inmates. Borgowiec fled to avoid witnessing the horrific event. He did not wish to see the prisoners take their final breaths. When Father Kolbe saw what was happening, he held out his weak arm, and death occurred almost immediately. He was forty-seven years old.

When Borgowiec returned to the cell, all four prisoners were dead. Later, he testified about Father Kolbe, "I'll never forget that gaze in his eyes." The priest's face was ecstatic, as though he were looking at some transcendent world.

Father Kolbe died on Thursday, August 14, 1941, the vigil of the feast of the Assumption of the Virgin Mary, an appropriate day for a man who lived and died in her honor and that of her son, Jesus Christ. His body was cremated the next day.

Chapter 16

The Road to Canonization

While most of us over the course of our lifetime come to know people whom we refer to as saints because of their holiness, few of these ever reach the level equal to those who are canonized, that is, officially recognized as saints. With the heroic death of Father Maximilian Kolbe in Auschwitz, the door to his path to becoming a canonized saint opened wide. The Church follows a process of several steps before declaring someone a saint. (See the Appendix.)

First, on May 12, 1955, Father Kolbe was called a Servant of God, which meant that a study of his life was undertaken. A positive report was sent to Rome. On January 30, 1969, Pope Paul VI declared Father Kolbe Venerable, which meant he had shown heroic virtue.

A miracle is required for the next step, beatification. In 1970, the Church accepted two miracles that occurred through Father Kobe's intercession. One involved Angela Testoni, a seamstress living in Sardinia, Italy, who was miraculously cured of tuberculosis. For many years she had suffered daily, and because her lungs and intestines were being eroded by the disease, the outlook was bleak. Her confessor recommended that she begin a prayer vigil to Father Maximilian Kolbe. She kept his picture under her pillow. In July 1949, the priest placed the picture on Angela's abdomen. Later that day her pain completely left her and she was able to eat normally. Three doctors confirmed the miraculous cure.

A second miracle occurred when Francis Ranier from Montegranario, Italy, was suffering from severe arthritis for many years. The disease led to the amputation of his right leg. After the surgeries, gangrene set it and infection spread through the man's body. He became delirious. On August 4, 1949, doctors said to expect death at any time. Ranier's wife and son prayed to Father

Kolbe and placed his picture under Ranier's pillow. Two days later, after a sound sleep, Ranier woke up calm, said he felt well, and ate. Both Angela Testoni and Francis Ranier lived for many years with no reoccurrence of their illness.

Other miracles have been attributed to Father Kolbe. His friend Father Bronislaus Stycxny contracted gangrene while he was imprisoned in the concentration camp in Dachau. He was scheduled for surgery to amputate his leg. If that were to happen, it would make him a cripple and he would likely have been gassed. He prayed to Father Kolbe and to another close friend to intercede for him. Later the gangrene disappeared totally unexpectedly. Released from Dachau while in his early fifties, he was sent to minister in the United States and was unable to testify in the canonization process in Rome.

As a result of the two approved miracles, Pope Paul VI beatified Father Kolbe on October 17, 1971, making him Blessed Maximilian Kolbe. Almost eleven years later, on October 10, 1982, Pope John Paul II proclaimed him a saint, a martyr of charity.

St. Maximilian is the patron saint of journalists, media communications, the family, the pro-life movement, prisoners, the chemically addicted, and amateur radio. His feastday is August 14, the day he entered eternal life. In 2000, the United States bishops designated Marytown in Libertyville, Illinois, as the National Shrine of Maximilian Kolbe. The site is a ministry of the Conventual Franciscan friars.

Appendix

Franciscek Gajowniczek

Born in Strachomin, Poland, on November 15, 1901, Franciscek (Francis) Gajowniczek became a farmer. He joined the Polish Army and served in World War I and II for a total of twenty-two years, eventually achieving the rank of sergeant. He was captured by the Gestapo in Zakopane, Poland, in 1939, and in July of 1940 became a Catholic political prisoner assigned number 26273. On October 8, he arrived at the Auschwitz concentration camp. At that time he and his wife, Helena, had two young sons.

On July 30, 1941, when Francis was forty-one years old, he was the last of ten prisoners selected to be placed in a starvation bunker. Brought back from the brink of death thanks to Father Maximilian Kolbe, he continued his daily struggles with life in the concentration camp. Now, though, he was emotionally drained and suffering from survivor's guilt. On October 23, 1944, Francis was transferred to another camp in Sachsenhasusen, Germany. This was a few months before the Soviet Union's Red Army liberated Auschwitz. On May 3, 1945, Francis and others were on the death march to Berlin when they were liberated by the United States Army.

Francis spent a total of five years, five months, and nine days in concentration camps. While in them, he amassed a number of survival miracles. Among them were the following:

- Became the only recorded survivor of the first 700 Polish deportees sent to Auschwitz.
- Barely escaped execution three times.
- Survived an almost certain death from typhus.
- Had a near death experience in which he witnessed a vision of Father Kolbe at the end of a bright road and heard him say that he would survive.

On returning to his home in Poland, Francis learned that his two sons were killed in 1945 during the Soviet bombardment of Poland. His weight had dropped from 165 pounds to 100 pounds. He and Helena moved to Brzeg, where she died in 1977. After Helena's death, he married his caretaker, Janina. Later he worked for the municipal government in Brzeg and served on their Board of Commissioners.

Francis traveled the world, speaking about surviving Auschwitz, the evils of war and totalitarianism and, most importantly, Father Kolbe's heroic works and martyrdom. Over the course of fifty years, he visited every country in Western Europe and made several tours in the United States. In 1989, he met with President George H. W. Bush at the White House.

Mr. Gajowniczek attended Father Kolbe's beatification and, at the age of eighty-one, his canonization. Francis died on March 13, 1995, when he was ninety-four years old, outliving Janina, who died in 1986. He was buried at Niepokalanow, one of three non-clergy buried there. The other two were Prince Jan Drucki-Lubecki, who had donated the property for Niepokalanow, and Dr. Jan Stankiewicz, who had offered his services free of charge to the friars at Niepokalanow.

The Process of Canonization

Early Christian martyrs were honored as saints. After persecutions ended, confessors who proclaimed the faith and then others who were recognized as holy were considered saints. There was no formal process; these people became saints by public acclaim based on what was believed to be credible information about their virtuous lives. Occasionally that information was discovered to be distorted or unfounded. The first documented papal canonization occurred in 993 when Pope John XV canonized St. Ulrich. In 1234, Pope Gregory IX established a formal process to investigate proposed candidates for sainthood to ensure that they practiced heroic virtue. In addition, the process called for posthumous miracles through the candidates' intercession as conclusive proof that they are united with God. Today the Congregation for the Causes of the Saints oversees the investigation of prospective saints.

The process of canonization can take centuries, for example, 450 years passed before Joan of Arc was declared a saint. However, in the case of Pope John Paul II, a waiver was granted of the five-year minimum wait before the start of the process, and he was canonized only nine years after his death. The process comprises the following phases:

Phase 1: The first step is at the diocesan or local level where the bishop initiates an investigation himself or from a petitioner (a parish, religious organization, or association). With permission from the Holy See a tribunal, headed by a Postulator is convened. At this stage, the person is known as the Servant of God. The tribunal interviews witnesses regarding the candidate's virtues and other specifics related to their state in life. It considers whether a miracle has been worked and studies the person's writings. A written report is drawn up and the bishop confers with other bishops and members of the public for their opinion. The report and documentation are sent to the Holy See in Rome.

Phase 2: The Congregation for the Causes of Saints hands the case to a Relator who oversees the Cause. The Relator and a commission of nine theologians investigate further. If the candidate is found to have lived a life of heroic virtue, the Congregation votes to proceed with the cause. When the pope approves, the candidate is declared Venerable.

Phase 3: For the title Blessed, a miracle must be attributed to a candidate. Martyrs, though, do not require a miracle. Miracles are investigated by five specialist doctors and two in-house experts. A miracle must be immediate, spontaneous and complete and cannot be explained or refuted by medical science. About forty to fifty cases are examined each year and only one-third of these are voted to be true miraculous healings.

Phase 4: Once another miracle is credited to the candidate, he or she can be proclaimed a saint by the pope. This means the person is with God. With the decree of canonization, a person is affirmed as a model to imitate and may be venerated. The saint may be added to the general calendar of the Church.

Although a canonization may take place in the saint's country, it usually occurs with great fanfare in the context of a papal Mass in St. Peter's Square in Rome. The basilica is decorated and illuminated, images of the saint are displayed, and church bells are rung. A canonization is a grand celebration for the Church.

Photographs

Maryanna Kolbe (circa 1905-1910), mother of Franciszek, Rajmund, and Jozef Kolbe.

In Zdunska Wola, Poland, on Monday, January 8, 1894, in a two-room, second-floor flat in this house, Rajmund Kolbe was born.

Boys' choir and orchestra in Pabianice. Rajmund is in the front row, extreme left; Jozef is in the front row, middle; Franciszek is in the last row, extreme left.

Saint Matthew's Parish Church in Pabianice where the child Rajmund Kolbe received the vision of the two crowns at the altar of Our Lady of Victory.

Brother Maksymilian Kolbe, second row, left, at the Seraphic College in Rome in 1914.

Maksymilian Maria Kolbe in the year of his ordination to the priesthood in Rome in 1918.

Niepokalanow's original chapel, constructed in 1927.

The beginning construction of the Niepokalanow Monastery, 1927-1928.

The Skyscraper, the minor seminary dormitory at Niepokalanow, circa 1929.

The Miraculous Medal.

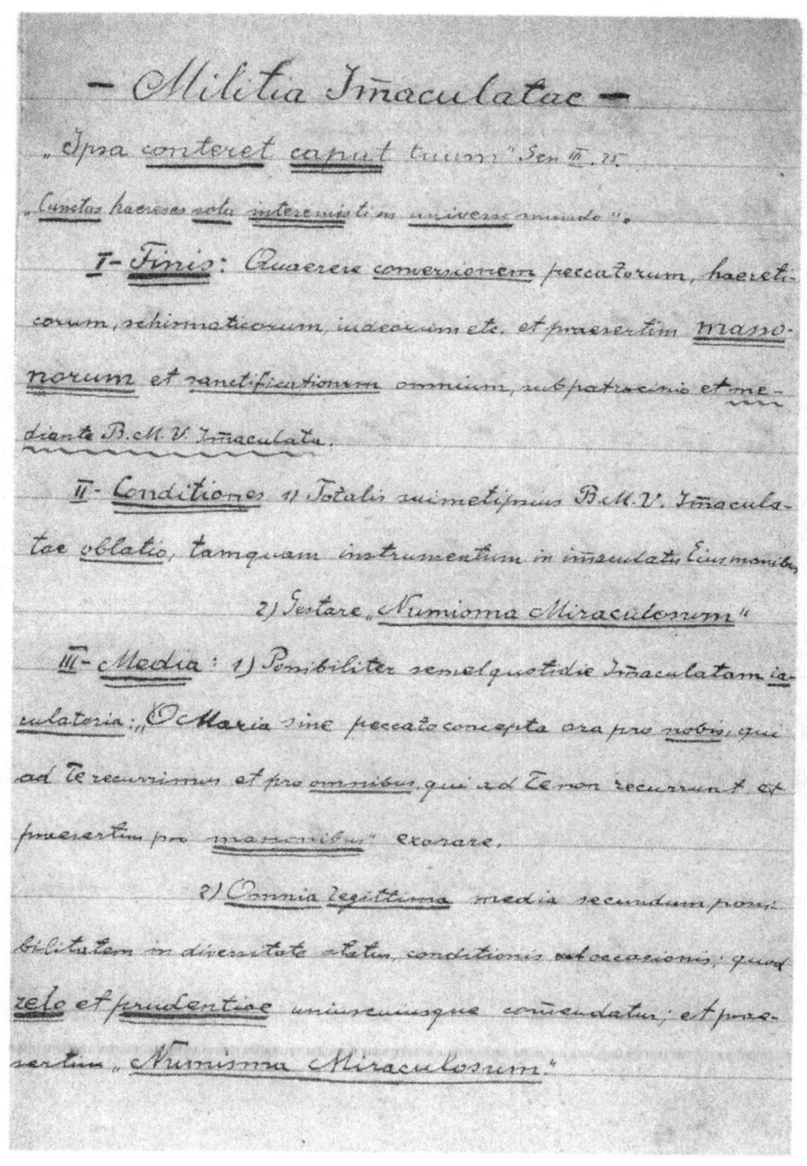

— Militia Immaculatae —

„Ipsa conteret caput tuum" Gen. III. 15.

„Cunctas haereses sola interemisti in universo mundo".

I - Finis: Quaerere conversionem peccatorum, haereticorum, schismaticorum, judaeorum etc. et praesertim massonorum et sanctificationem omnium, sub patrocinio et mediante B.M.V. Immaculata.

II - Conditiones 1) Totalis suimetipsius B.M.V. Immaculatae oblatio, tamquam instrumentum in immaculatis Eius manibus.

2) Gestare „Numisma Miraculosum"

III - Media: 1) Possibiliter semel quotidie Immaculatam ejaculatoria: „O Maria sine peccato concepta ora pro nobis, qui ad Te recurrimus et pro omnibus, qui ad Te non recurrunt et praesertim pro massonibus" exorare.

2) Omnia legittima media secundum possibilitatem in diversitate status, conditionis et occasionis; quod zelo et prudentiae uniuscuiusque commendatur; et praesertim „Numisma Miraculosum".

The original Statute of the MI, handwritten in Latin by St. Maximilian Maria Kolbe.

One of the major presses at Niepokalanow.

Friars preparing *The Knight* for mailing in Poland.

The Mugensai no Sono community, circa 1933.

Brother Seweryn Dagis (center) and assistant, typesetting Japanese characters in Nagasaki, circa 1930.

A current photograph of Mugensai no Sono. Mount Hikosan is in the background.

Brother Zeno Zebrowski from 1945 until his death on Saturday, April 24, 1982, ministered to Japanese orphans.

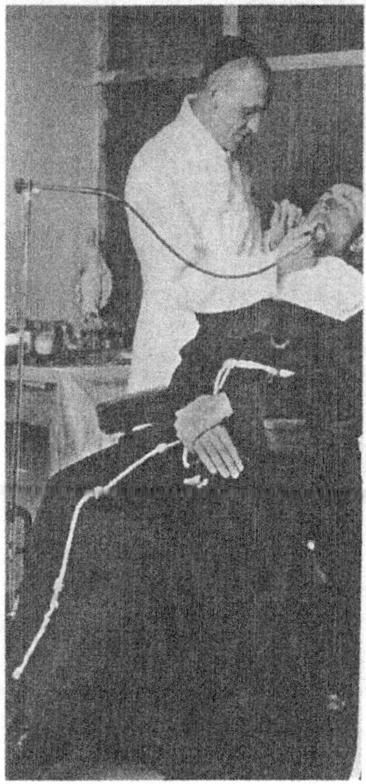

Father Maksymilian with the friars of the Niepokalanow fire department.

The Niepokalanow dental service.

Friars sculpting statues of the Immaculata.

Father Maksymilian at Zakopane, the Polish Alps, during a curative rest, circa 1936-1939.

Niepokalanow monastic community, circa 1938-1939. Father Maksymilian, with beard, stands in right center of the sixth row.

The Niepokalanow radio began broadcasting on December 11, 1938.

Br. Manswet Marczewski at microphone.

Members of the Wehrmacht garrison housed at Niepokalanow.

Father Maksymilian. Circa 1940.

Some of the refugees housed at Niepokalanow from 1939 to 1945.

At the request of the Wehrmacht Lieutenant at Niepokalanow, this photo was taken in January 1941, shortly before Father Maksymilian's arrest on Monday, February 17, 1941. Brother Iwo stands on the right.

Drawing of Kolbe volunteering to take the place of a prisoner condemned to die in reprisal for an escapee who had not been found. By Polish artist Prof. Miecislaus Koscielniak, a fellow prisoner of Kolbe's at Auschwitz.

Auschwitz's "Block of Death," where Kolbe died.

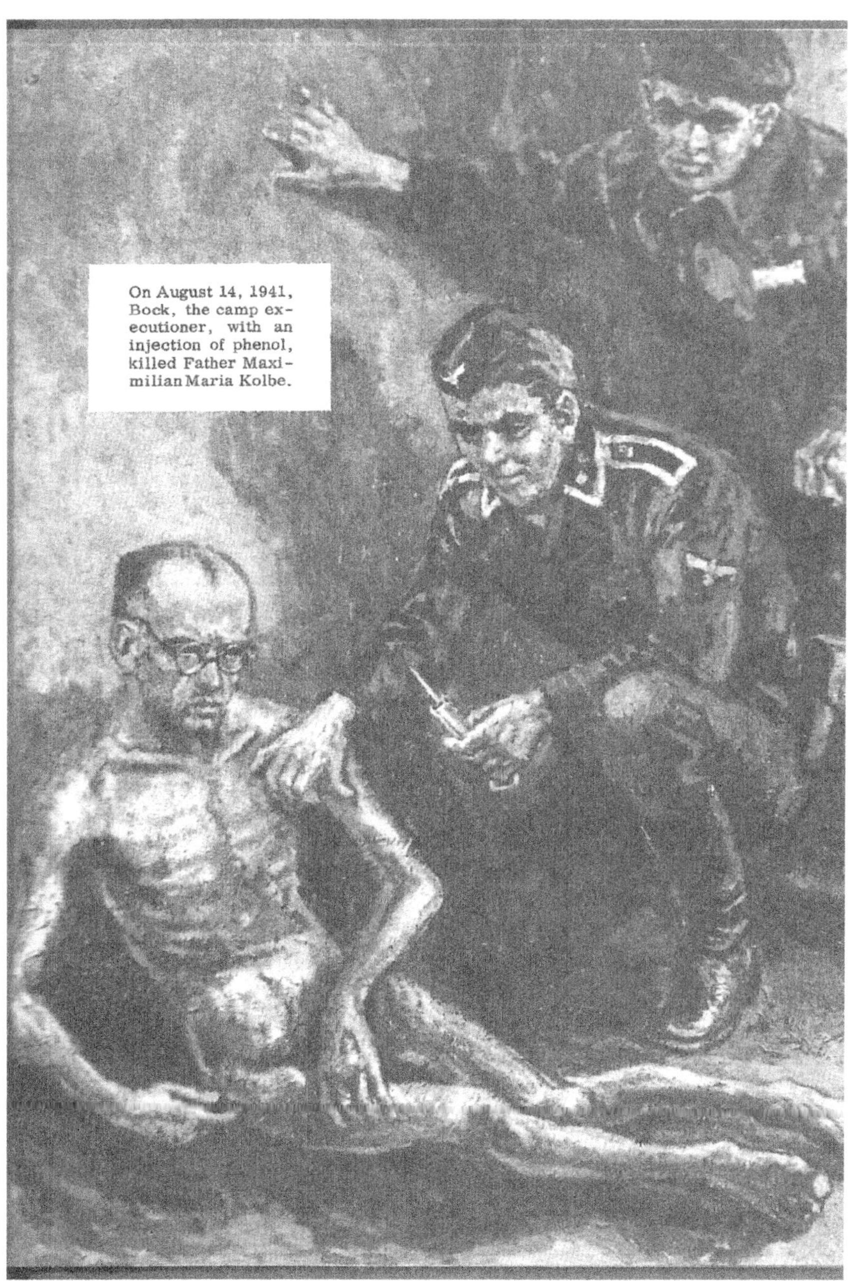

Drawing by Polish artist M. Koscielniak

Nr. 510/1941 (508) C

Auschwitz, den 19. August 1941.

Der Pfarrer Rajmund Kolbe, römisch-katholisch

wohnhaft Niepokalanow Kreis Sochaczew

ist am 14. August 1941 um 12 Uhr 50 Minuten

in Auschwitz, Kasernenstraße verstorben.

Der Verstorbene war geboren am 7. Januar 1894

in Zdunska Wola

(Standesamt — Nr. —)

Vater: Julius Kolbe

Mutter: Marie Kolbe geborene Dabrowski, wohnhaft in Krakau

~~Der Verstorbene war nicht verheiratet~~

Eingetragen auf ~~mündliche~~ — schriftliche Anzeige des Arztes Doktor Schwela in Auschwitz vom 14. August 1941

~~Der Anzeigende~~

~~Vorgelesen, genehmigt und unterschrieben~~

Die Übereinstimmung mit dem Erstbuch wird beglaubigt.

Auschwitz, den 19.8. 1941.

Der Standesbeamte
In Vertretung

Der Standesbeamte
In Vertretung
Grabner

Todesursache: Myocardinsufficiens

Eheschliessung de Verstorbenen am — in —

(Standesamt — Nr. —).

Cause of death was listed a heart failure.

A recent photograph of the Auschwitz starvation bunker.

The grave of Franciszek Gajowniczek (Tuesday, October 1, 1901 - Monday, March 13, 1995). Franciszek Gajowniczek was the fellow countryman for whom Father Maksymilian sacrificed his life at Auschwitz. Franciszek Gajowniczek is buried in the Niepokalanow Friary Cemetery.

The Immaculate Conception Minor Basilica at Niepokalanow, built by the friars between 1948-1954.

The canonization Mass for Father Maksymilian Maria Kolbe on Sunday, October 10, 1982 on Saint Peter's Square.

Niepokalanow's original chapel after recent renovation. The Basilica is in the background. Photograph taken in July, 2001.

Interior of the Niepokalanow chapel (built in 1927) after recent renovation. Photograph taken in July of 2001.

Inventions and Illustrations

The following pages are taken from *The Writings of St. Maximilian Maria Kolbe*, Volume II. These are English translations of his original narratives describing his proposed space craft and electronic devices, as well as his personal drawings and mathematical calculations. To what pinnacle he could have propelled to in the field of science or math will never be known because he chose, instead, to soar to the height of sainthood, which he succeeded to through his martyrdom in Auschwitz.

1386 The Etherplane and Other Devices

MI

Rome, before December 3, 1918[1]

*I. Etherplane

Problem.

When I heard in a physics class, 4 or 5 years ago at the Gregorian University, from the Rev. Fr. Cesare Goretti, that there is a safe limit beyond which, when firing—for example a cannon—and taking into consideration the force of the blast, the ball will not reach, it occurred to me to wonder if that limit was absolutely safe, and whether somehow it might be possible to get beyond it. I thought that if that ball, being already near the limit, were to explode and then shoot out a fragment that goes beyond that limit, and if one increased the number of blasts, it could send the last fragment of the ball much farther beyond the limit. The observation of fireworks helped me in this. All that is obvious.

But, I thought, if that last fragment were a craft, which in the earlier blasts lost very little matter at great speed, and if one multiplied the blasts, then, quite independently of the environment, relying purely on the law of equality of action and reaction, as it lost some, it could progress with what was left.

So I thought of the possibility of an etherplane, an aircraft for reaching beyond the earth to the moon, to other planets, assuming that an extraordinary increase in speed were possible as the gravitational force of the earth decreased, or even more by using the gravitational pull [of the planets].

Considering all the aspects of such an extraordinary voyage together, two classes of difficulties emerge spontaneously, that is, concerning *the craft and the man* who travels in it. The second issue has mainly to do with biology. Three principal concerns, perhaps: one concerning the attraction of bodies and consequently one's abnormal state according to one's different positions among the stars, which does

* Original text in Italian.

1 Fr. Maximilian took his research in physics quite seriously and had intended to publish it in the Italian journal *La scienza per tutti*, based in Milan. From the editor of that journal, Fr. Maximilian received the following letter, dated December 3, 1918: "Dear Mr. Rajmund Dąbrowski, Via S. Teodoro 41F, Rome. Given that we usually avoid 'projects' in favor of already constructed inventions, we would like to inform you that for our part we put forward only one condition: that the material prove worthy of publication to our Technical Committee. Usually, contributors to our feature 'Devices and Inventions' are content with the free advertising that comes with the publication of their invention. If you wish to publish something under special conditions, please let us know and we shall gladly consider your proposal. We look forward to reading it. Yours truly. *La scienza per tutti*, [illegible signature]."

not seem insurmountable to me, considering that even on this earth we find ourselves in different positions; experimentation would show that.

The second and third would have to do with *lack of air* and with *pressure*. The issue could be dealt with by taking along liquefied air or oxygen, or purifying the air inside the aircraft by using plants or in some other way. Then the pressure would remain the same, assuming that the aircraft is hermetically sealed and carries air inside with the required pressure. An armored body, possibly made of steel, would prevent the whole aircraft from exploding because of lack of external pressure. Issues to do with the lack of light, heat and food would not be serious, considering that electricity and other necessities can be easily carried onboard.

The main difficulties would concern the traveler, but the aircraft may, for initial trials, go unmanned, on an automated mission there and back. And if it is equipped with photographic, phonographic, thermographic devices, etc., it could provide a very good report of its journey.

The *difficulty* we need to overcome has to do with *motion*, that is, the way we can make an aircraft move in empty or near empty space (at least as far as air is concerned).

For all crafts rely on some type of resistance: While it turns, a wheel does not move the wagon unless it touches the ground; a propeller does not advance a ship unless it touches water, an airplane unless it touches air. In our case, what we lack is precisely this resistance and that is the *main problem* to be dealt with for an etherplane. For that reason, it seems that we need to change the principle of propulsion, or rather go to the more general principle and apply it differently, without pistons, wheels or propellers. The very general principle regarding force is that every action has an equal and opposite reaction. We should therefore use reaction, starting with action.

$$(+)\,F_1 = (-)\,F_2$$
$$m_1\gamma_1 = m_2\gamma_2$$
$$m_1 s_1 = m_2 s_2$$

The equation contains two elements: that is, mass and acceleration (or speed or space), the product of which is the same for both sides. Yet elements can change, so we should use the part where mass equals the mass of the craft with the acceleration afforded by the force of the blast, losing then minimum mass with the greatest speed:

$$M\,\gamma = \underset{\wedge}{m}\,\underset{\vee}{\gamma}$$

That would be *the principle*. To obtain a major blast force more easily, the combustion chamber could be made so that it breaks open instantly and automatically only when the *desired tension* is achieved.

More concretely [figs. 1–5].[2]

Another difficulty may come from rocks floating around in space. To avoid collisions, a compass and a gravitational field (weight) might serve to some extent, for they could automatically steer the craft.

These seem to me the main difficulties concerning the aircraft and the human traveler. The main issue, that is, about the motion of the craft, seems to me sufficiently solved (resolved), and so at least we could first send the aircraft equipped only with devices, using rigorous calculations to determine its exact route and make sure that it comes back automatically. Once it is back, we could look at the difference between our forecast and facts and, having eliminated possible flaws, we could send it out to a greater distance and then back to examine the result again. Once it appears that the aircraft is safe and that animals placed into it for the first launches are all right, a journey may be ventured without endangering human life. The question really requires much testing, studying… and money.

II

The same principle of precision of the device might be usefully applied to our *airplanes*, thereby greatly increasing their speed. It would seem that even machinery could do without pistons and use this principle, for instance [fig. 6].

And the same could work for automobiles, specifically, with the wheels, because the first way, as in the etherplane and airplane, would perhaps not be so convenient for […].[3]

Etherplane[4]

Namely, a craft for going up into the ether, that is, to the planets and even the distant stars. Apart from the physiological difficulties of the travelers, which do not seem insurmountable, it seems to me that even the problem of propulsion (the main issue) can be solved. It is true that in order to move away from ground, water and air, one can use neither a wheel nor a propeller, for these absolutely require some sort of resistance. We should therefore use a different principle, or rather, apply differently the general principle of force, namely that "*each action has an equal and opposite reaction.*" By exploiting reaction and reducing action, we could possibly achieve mo-

2 In the original there are several sketches and drawings, some quite difficult to read and understand.

3 Obscure word.

4 The paragraph that follows is possibly the beginning of Fr. Maximilian's final draft on his research on the etherplane, because the original presents a very careful graphic layout and meticulous handwriting.

tion without resistance, as in the painful rebound that an inexperienced hunter or soldier feels when shooting, which is a reaction caused by the action of the bullet blasting out. This action (reduced by the recoil of the gun) and reaction of the gun or cannon do not depend on the mediums that surround them, or rather, without them they move even farther. It seems that this would fit well [...].[5]

If possible, perpetual motion understood in this sense:

1. Assuming the *existence* of sources of forces;
2. Assuming the possibility of their indefinite duration (lasting indefinitely);
3. Assuming a different susceptibility among the forces of different mediums to action, and consequently a diversity of intensity, which does not coincide with the lines of the forces: that is, a deviation of the lines of force from the less susceptible medium to the more susceptible medium, and equilibration in the equal medium (homogeneous, with regard to that force). Hence the possibility of an indefinitely lasting mode for points that are sensitive to these kinds of forces, distributed so that they find themselves sometimes in a more and sometimes in a less intense field, so they may first be suppressed and then suppress the others [figs. 7–13].

1387 Telegraphic and Recording Devices

Lviv–Krakow, 1907–1919[1]

The undersigned ventures to present to the Royal Ministry[2] his own personal inventions:

1. A writing telegraph;
2. A device that records speech and the sounds of nature;
3. A telegraph in which at one station one can only speak, while at a second station a device receives and records. The undersigned also asks for a sympathetic examination and evaluation of these inventions as to whether they are practicable.

5 This sentence is left unfinished.

1 Fr. Maximilian signed this as a "12th grade high school student." He was a high school senior in the years 1907–1908. He must have worked on this manuscript at least until 1919 (cf. *KW* 980 U, October 20, "At work there: MI, inventions, putting things in order"); it seems, however, that he was never able to complete his research, because his health and his Marian activity absorbed more and more of his time.

2 Fr. Maximilian was, on more than one occasion, interested in publishing his research (cf. *KW* 34; 54). However, there is no evidence that this writing was ever actually sent to ministerial authorities.

1. I have two types of writing telegraphs: a simple one, and a second that writes more quickly and is more complex. Neither of these devices writes on tape, but on paper, such as [...],[3] and they both write letters, not signs.

2. The device that records speech and the sounds of nature can (a) record human speech (this device also records *periods* and *commas*); (b) record the sounds of nature, such as a loud noise, the howling of the wind, the roar of the rain, a crash, etc. (the device records, for example, a loud noise using the words "loud noise," howling using the word "howling," etc.); (c) record musical notes sung in songs or played, without omitting to indicate, by using letters of the alphabet, "piano," "forte," and so on; (d) reproduce the sounds of animals, etc.

3. The telegraph—into which one need only speak for the device at the other station to record or speak, or record and reproduce—comes from the fusion of the first two machines. Therefore, the device can record and play back both the call of an animal and the sounds of nature.

Rajmund Kolbe
12th grade high school student

1. Simple Writing Telegraph

At the Broadcasting Station [figs. 1–3][4]

The entire apparatus is composed of a cylinder (d).[5] The lower end of a needle touches the wax in the grooves, while the other end is connected to one of the pins by means of a spring (to be able to move more freely). Above it there is a small plate connected to the second pin.

Prior to telegraphing, the cylinder needs to be loaded. To do that, we place a cartridge on it (a small tube, on the upper side of which are the needle tips that align with the grooves of the small drum). A single set of alphabet letters on the small drum runs around the cylinder only once, so we can move the cartridge along the small drum (this can be done using a clock mechanism). Instead of the small drum, there could be a disc similar to a gramophone's. In that case, the cartridge must be a disc and must have all the letters (a few sets of alphabet letters). In the cylinder, there could also be a cartridge with more than one set of alphabet letters (as many as there are in the cylinder). If we want to telegraph, we press down, one after the other, in the cartridge, the needles for the letters desired (in this way, the cylinder can rotate on

3 Drawing of a piece of paper with horizontal lines.
4 In the original, there are also 23 drawings, mostly sketches and quite small.
5 Letters of the alphabet are explained below.

itself). Backtracking is *not possible*. Marks will be left imprinted onto the wax in the grooves. When the needle (c) slides along the small drum and encounters a groove, it will drop down, while the second end will touch the plate and engage the electric current. Then the needle springs up and stops the flow of current.

At the Receiving Station [figs. 4–6]

The device at the receiving station consists of two horseshoe-shaped electromagnets—between which is located a narrow cylinder, on which are placed rubber letters and punctuation marks—and a "Nefa" hammer, and through this, paper is fed. The two ends of the paper are joined together and the paper passes through two cylinders, one of which has a small, toothed wheel, which is simply a clock mechanism. Both small wheels connect two arms at both ends of the cylinders.

In both stations, the clock mechanisms work *in time with each other*, so on both stations the letters too work in time with each other, and when at the bottom part of the first station there is any one letter, in the same place in the second there will also be the same letter. It follows that, when the electric current is running for the duration of time corresponding to a given letter, at the receiving station, the magnet will attract the Nefa hammer and, since a piece of material soaked in ink or other liquid suitable for the purpose is attached to a part of the letter cylinder, the hammer will press the paper against the wetted letter and the letter will be printed. The hammer, repositioned at the bottom, will free the toothed wheel from the stop hook "i" and allow it to move by one tooth (which corresponds to the space established for one letter), while the paper will move for the space of a letter and leave white space under the hammer for a new letter. When the paper has made a full revolution and returns to the page seam (under the Nefa hammer), the paper will shift to one side along with the cylinders, with the help of the clock mechanism. When the printing finally reaches the end of the cylinder, a new sheet of paper will have to be fed in (for the first one will already have been filled). Sheets of paper of different lengths and widths may be used. If the sheet is narrow, it will need to be placed not at the top but at the bottom of the cylinder, because when the cylinder reaches the end it will stop by itself. In the event that we wish to have a shorter sheet of paper, we can shorten the little arm that connects the cylinders (given that it can slide inside the cylinder, for example [fig. 7]), and when we want to place a longer sheet of paper, we can lengthen it. If we want to have a very large sheet of paper, we can place the small drums at a greater distance from each other. If we want to have a long and narrow piece of paper (as it often happens), we can position the toothed wheel, driven by the clock mechanism, perpendicular to the one shown in the drawing, and secure the connection of the cylinders (the little arm) by a metal strap with holes corresponding to the teeth of the wheel [fig. 8], while the toothed wheel will push along the small drums with the paper (when the cap allows it). This wheel may also be used in the former model (as in the drawing) to push along, but in that case it will have to have yet another tooth that hooks the strap only when the whole sheet of paper has already been printed on for its entire length. In this case, however, the teeth of the wheel will not move the strap but will be placed next to the wheel so as to be moved by the perpendicular wheel. These teeth will have to be shaped as shown: [fig. 9].

The same thing may be done in reverse, swapping the perpendicular wheels and folding the strap (in this case composed of parts joined together): [fig. 10] so that it can move freely. To ensure that the device stops on its own after filling a sheet of paper, we could add to the strap with holes two wires that divide; in which case the teeth will be unable to push the strap [fig. 11]. Also, it would be good to make it possible for some small drums to be loaded simultaneously at the broadcasting station and then placed under the needle one after the other. The machine could be made to move so fast that a telegram written in full letters could reach its destination more quickly than the ones written with conventional signs, because the Nefa hammer can operate very fast.

Rajmund Kolbe
12th grade high school student

2. [Compound Telegraph]

The compound telegraph consists of several small drums connected together. With this telegraph it is not necessary, as in the previous one, to wait one revolution for a second identical letter, because, for example, when the telegraph is on the small drum, we divide the alphabet into four parts and start the alphabets on the small drums one after the other: in the first, from the first letter; in the second, from the second column of letters; in the third, from the third; and the fourth, from the fourth column of letters. In this way, on the fourth part of an alphabet we can have the whole alphabet distributed over all the four small drums.

At the Broadcasting Station

At the broadcasting station, we proceed as in the previous telegraph, the only difference being that each needle of the cartridge represents four letters, while the cartridge can rotate on itself more freely. If we want to enter a letter by taking it from the next small drum, we widen the slot of the last letter of the small drum by half of the space of the letter that follows, directly advancing the needle by half of the space of the letter that follows and then pushing it back in place. When we want to get a letter from the third drum, we push the needle for the entire space of the letter that follows; when we want to take it from the fourth, we push for the space of a letter and a half. Since, in doing this, *time* passes, we must take it into account in determining the next letter. The time may be reduced with more rapid movement of the "shifter" at the receiving station. After the small drum (cylinder) has been loaded, it must be placed under the needle. (As in the first telegraph, so also in the second: to ensure that the letters are printed with greater precision, a small spring may be placed at the transmitting station, as shown in letter *g* in the illustration.)

At the Receiving Station [fig. 12]

a: shifter of the small drum that moves the small bar *z z* by means of the teeth and which, next to *z*, will appear as follows: [fig. 13];

u: small bars that connect the shifter with the axis of the small drum and set it in motion;

n n: electromagnets;

m: small compound drum;

k: paper on cylinders;

p: power switch;

s: cap;

r: small cylinder into which fits the cap;

t: wheels that turn the small drum (one sets the other in motion, and the latter activates the small drum);

i: wheel that activates the lever;

h: as well as the axis of the lever;

h: lever;

z c: clamps that hold the engaged lever *h* raised off the tooth of the wheel *i*;

c: wheels that set in motion the shifter *a*.

[figs. 14–15]

a, a^1, and a^2 are also the outer walls, while the whole cap is a good conductor. When the cap is raised, the current flows and the Nefa letter hammer is attracted by the magnet. At the same instant, the second hammer will hit magnet *n* and close the cap. The current cannot flow through the cap and circulates around part *k* of the cap. Disc *2h* and *h*, through which the second arm of *r* will be positioned between the teeth *b*. When current flows longer, the wheel *i*, too, if arm *r* pauses briefly in the teeth, moves to an area where there are no teeth. When arm *r* remains there longer, wheel *i* raises it with its tooth and places it in clamp *c*. When the current flow is interrupted, the second Nefa hammer engages and, with the help of the small bar, lifts the arms of *c*; then, the clamp also lets go of the arm of *r*, which, by the aid of the spring, is immediately lowered. When (in order to print the letters) the upper arm of *r* is released from the teeth *b* placed at the top, the lower arm will engage teeth *b* positioned at the bottom. In this way shifter *a* connected with *b* will be prevented from moving while letters are being printed. The paper is arranged as in the simple telegraph, but it is pushed along. Next to the telegraph machines, we may seal a telegram with the help of a small box, into which the printed sheet is dropped. The bottom of this box can bend (inside the box). Before sealing, the edge of the paper may be pressed down onto a strip of paper soaked in glue, or if the paper had been glued previously it can be moistened with water. Finally, the bottom folds up and the telegram is glued [figs. 16–17].

Rajmund Kolbe
12th grade high school student

3. A Device That Records Speech and the Sounds of Nature [fig. 18]

The main part of the device consists of a small tape and a needle connected to a wire that perforates a thin strip of wax or other similar material, hard, but that can melt easily. Current coming from an electric battery heats the wire (so that it can move more freely). The vibrations caused on the tape are imprinted onto the wax strip. But given that such vibrations are relatively weak, a wire can be attached onto the lever, the lower arm of which would be set in motion by the needle. Depending on the marks that have been imprinted, similar metal marks may be made and the corresponding letters placed onto both the connection elements: [fig. 19].

When a sign, which matches any one letter, moves along the tape and comes under a matching metal mark, the latter (overlapping the opening) will drop in and immediately snap out (with the help of a spring or a clock mechanism). After piercing the wax, the sign will go forward and imprint its letter unto the paper, or (given that the letters will be stamped at uneven distances between them) it will pierce the ribbon of soft material that moves forward, while on the punched tape the letter will come under a bunch of bristles dipped in ink, which, holding it firmly, will pass through the opening and print the given letter on the paper [fig. 20].

When one speaks and makes a short pause, the hot wire can melt some wax at a point; when the pause is longer, the hole produced by the melting will be wider and the iron wire will drop a little. Marks made in this way may be used to indicate commas and stops.

In order to obtain the written sounds of nature and animals, after choosing a suitable sign, we could make a similar one in metal and connect to it not only a letter but whole words, for example: loud noise, barking of a dog, etc.

The device for writing musical notes works in the same way, except that in this case the paper should have the music staves already printed, while the metallic notes will be either higher or lower, depending on the pitch. The same note sung or played softly will leave a similar, though slightly different mark, so next to it we could add an "f[orte]" or "p[iano]," etc.

This may be applied to all the disturbances produced by the vibration of the tape.

While sending a telegram, we can telegraph the letters corresponding to a given voice, while on the second station, we will read on the writing telegraph and we will hear them from the apparatus.

When at one station we talk into the device, the device can imprint the letters; these can load the small drum; the next station will receive a written telegram, the telegraph will write, while the device will reproduce [the sounds].

Rajmund Kolbe
12th grade high school student

[Observations on the Telegraph That Records Speech and the Sounds of nature]

Voice can be rendered in the form of short dashes engraved onto gramophone discs. According to these dashes, one could, after hardening some metal discs, cast an alphabet of dash-based characters. The device, in fact, is made with the help of the latter.

In the dash-based alphabet, characters are connected, by means of a lever, with the characters of the alphabet consisting of letters. The lever lowers and raises the dash-based characters, so that the other lever, which retrieves the dashes, may be pushed farther down. Each character has a spring. When the lever lowers, the characters press against the dashes that were created, for instance, by speaking. When the groove matches the bump (convex) that is on the character, the character is lowered and the letter-based character is raised up and prints the letter on the disc [fig. 21]. The axis of the lever depends on the depth of the groove that is on the tape. On the small disk, letters are arranged at uneven distances; therefore, they engage the printer. The printer consists of a hammer-shaped brush (soaked in ink or in other suitable liquid), which repeatedly strikes the disk that passes beneath it. When a perforated letter comes under it, the end of the brush passes in part through the opening and prints the letter on the paper that is located under the disc. The course covered is now greater, so it remains attached to a tooth of the small wheel and pushes the paper forward one space to the next letter.

Even the sounds of animals and nature produce matching dashes. The characters of these dashes are connected with the characters of the corresponding words or expressions. For example, the device reproduces noise with the term "noise," the mewing of a cat with the phrase "the cat meows," etc.

Having instead the corresponding word with impressed letters (for example, when you send a telegram), you can do the reverse: retrieve the voice that matches that word. Therefore, even in the telegraph, when one speaks into the broadcasting station, the unit of the receiving station, which has a small drum with dash-based characters, will not only record the words, but also print the corresponding dashes, with the help of which the gramophone will play the words and voices in general, while the device [...].[6] When free characters form a word that indicates some voices, the characters, since they match the corresponding holes, can come down on their own, impress a dash-based character, and print [...].[7]

[Observations on the Writing Telegraph, Simple or Compound]

The *simple writing telegraph* consists of a cylinder and a needle. Along the whole cylinder, there runs a groove made in wax or other soft material. With the help of a small spring, the upper end of the needle is connected to one of the pins [of the cylinder]. Before using the telegraph, you load the small drum. Loaded in this way, the cylinder is placed under the needle and starts moving. When the lower end of the needle, by sliding along the groove of the cylinder, meets and falls into a recess, the upper end comes in contact with a small foil connected with the second pin [of the cylinder] and engages the current, until the lower end has moved out of the recess.

At the Receiving Station

The device consists of a Nefa hammer shaped as in our illustration [fig. 22], by a narrow cylinder for letters, which has on its cylindrical surface an alphabet and punctuation marks, and by two cylinders for paper. The paper passes through both cylinders and its ends are joined to form a tube, while its side margins reach to the ends [of the cylinders]. The cylinders are joined by a folding arm (which can be either shortened or lengthened depending on the size of the paper). The characters-letters that are on the wheel match the grooves of the same letters in the broadcasting station. When the current is turned on at the broadcasting station, the Nefa hammer presses the paper that is above it against the stationary letter of the wheel of letters, which moves in a jerking motion, like the wheel next to the balance mechanism of a clock. When at any given time the current stops, it pushes back the Nefa hammer, which going back to its original position moves the toothed wheel, which moves the paper cylinders forward by one tooth, and by doing that leaves a blank space on the paper for the next letter. When the paper has completed its revolution (for a certain number of letters), the cylinders move to one side along with the paper to the space corresponding to the height of a letter, and then paper starts to go round again. The sheet of paper may be printed either following the turning of the cylinder, or lengthwise.

The *compound writing telegraph* differs from the previous one in the fact that it has a greater number of small drums connected together (but not many), so one may telegraph more swiftly. At the broadcasting end, the unit is exactly the same, differing only in terms of loading. Each needle in the cartridge is assigned a letter.

The cartridge consists of a movable ring, marked with the letters that match given locations on the cylinder, and of a small fixed handle with (*a*) some small buttons for *1*, *2*, and *a* of this small drum. The movable ring rotates with the cylinder that moves in jerks (like the wheel next to the balance mechanism of the clock). In addition to the rotational movement, the cylinder is pushed forward toward the small handle. The letters are placed on the ring as shown in the illustration [fig. 23]. Each alphabet, therefore, has all its letters around it. To see the main table better (in accordance with which the needles are engaged), a small frame is placed next to the ring.

1388 The Number of Operations in Mathematics

Krakow-Grodno, 1919-1924[1]

When I was still in school, I had heard that in mathematics the operations are "7, only 7, and cannot possibly be more" (with the exception of differential calculus), namely: addition, subtraction, multiplication, division, exponentiation, roots and logarithms. However, it did not seem to me that mathematics was thereby anointing the number 7, because in general the limits of this science are lost in infinity. I submitted my arguments to my professor, who the next day declared, "so far, the operations are 7."

That happened 13 years ago. Many other occupations prevented me from delving deeper into the matter; so here are a few short remarks now.

By operation, I mean a way of combining and dividing numbers. Therefore, I am not for the moment speaking of differential or integral calculus, and I am even omitting the calculation of logarithms. I will confine myself therefore to addition, multiplication, and the exponentiation, on the one hand, and subtraction, division, and roots on the other.

Examining even superficially to the relationship between these operations, I have come to the conclusion that these are not all the operations possible [...].[2]

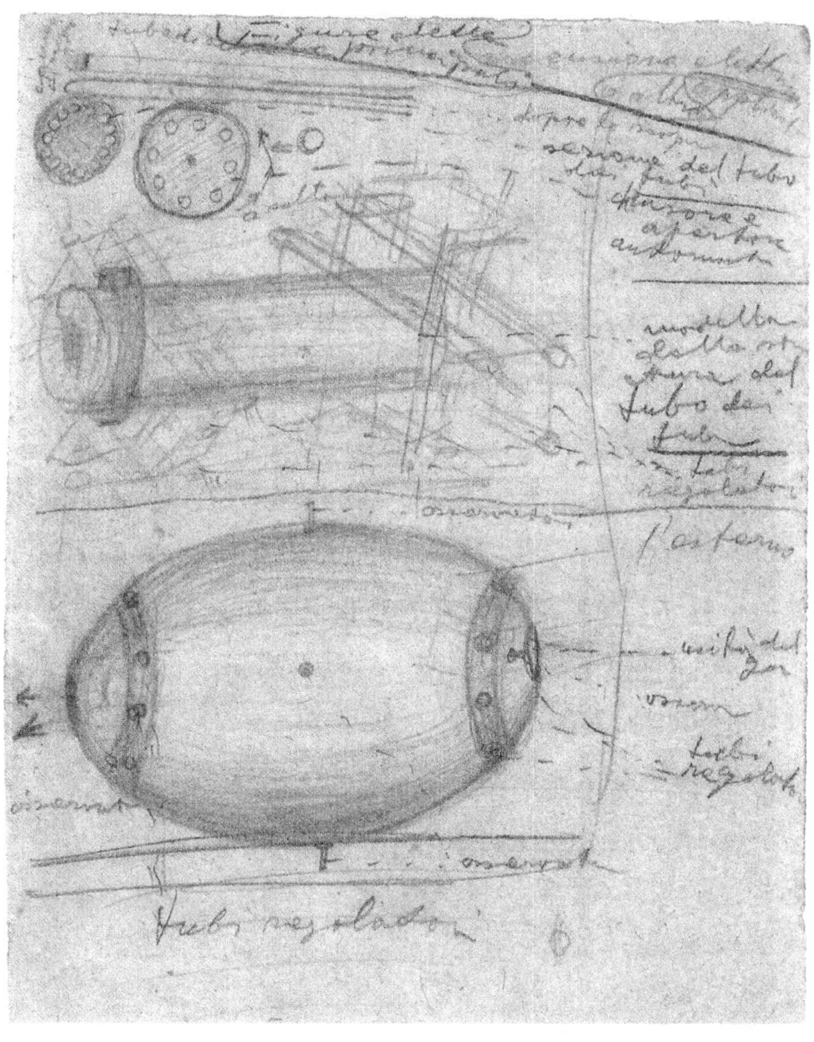

"Etherplane: Namely, a craft for going up into the ether, that is, to the planets and even the distant stars" (*KW* 1386). The exterior of the spacecraft, which is elliptical in shape, features a "armored body, made of steel." In the middle of the figure and at the ends you will notice observation windows. At one end there is the gas exhaust, which is connected with the "combustion chamber." Regulating pipes for checking the direction of the spacecraft are included in the drawings.

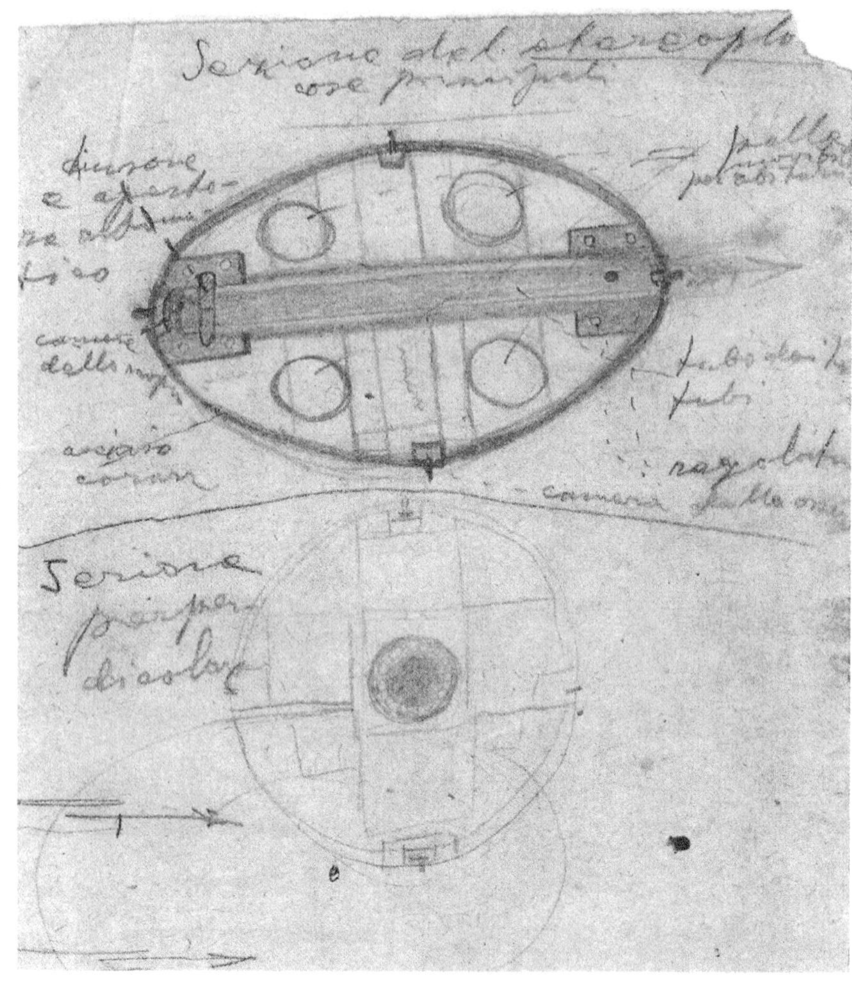

The inside of the etherplane shows, along the central axis, a collection of tubes, connected with the "combustion chamber," for the discharge of propulsion gases. Inside the spacecraft, there is a "movable sphere for the living quarters" of the astronauts.

Fr. Maximilian's notes concerning the etherplane. This page begins with the statement, "To obtain a major blast force more easily, the combustion chamber could be made so that it breaks open instantly and automatically only when the *desired tension* is achieved."

I

Telegraf prosty.

Na stacyi nadającej

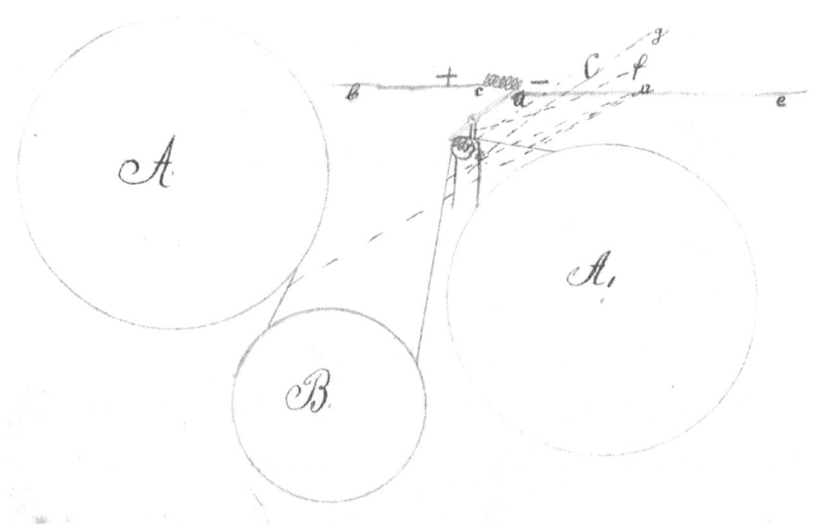

"Simple writing telegraph, at the broadcasting station."

Ośmielam się przedłożyć Wysokiemu C.K. Ministerium moje samodzielne pomysły:

1) telegraf piszący,

2) aparat zapisujący mowę i głosy natury,

3) telegraf, w którym na stacyi można tylko mówić, a na drugiej stacyi będzie to zapisywał odbierał aparat;

i prosić o łaskawe zbadanie i oszacowanie ich pod względem praktyczności.

1) Telegrafów piszących mam dwa rodzaje: jeden prosty, drugi zaś piszący prędzej i więcej złożony. Obydwa te aparaty nie piszą na wstędze, ale na kartce papieru np: i piszą literami, nie zaś znaczkami.

2). Aparat zapisujący mowę i głosy natury a może być zapa-ratem zapisującym mowę ludzką (Aparat ten oznacza także kropki i przecinki). b) aparatem zapisującym głosy natury np: huk, trzask, wycie wiatru, plusk deszczu i.t.d (aparat ten zapisuje np: huk słowem „huk" wycie słowem „wycie" i.t.d) c) aparatem zapisującym nuty ze śpiewu lub granych (melodyj) utworów (nie pomijając zaznaczać literami „piano" „forte" i.t.d) d) aparatem oddającym głosy zwierząt i.t.d.

3) Telegraf do którego należy tylko mówić, aby na drugiej stacyi aparat to zapisał lub wypowiedział, albo też zapisał i odtworzył go, jej połączeniem dwóch pierwszych aparatów. A więc i

Rajmund Kolbe (later Maximilian) describes his personal inventions (*KW* 1387): "1. A writing telegraph;
2. A device that records speech and the sounds of nature; 3. A telegraph in which at one station one can only speak, while at a second station a device receives and records."

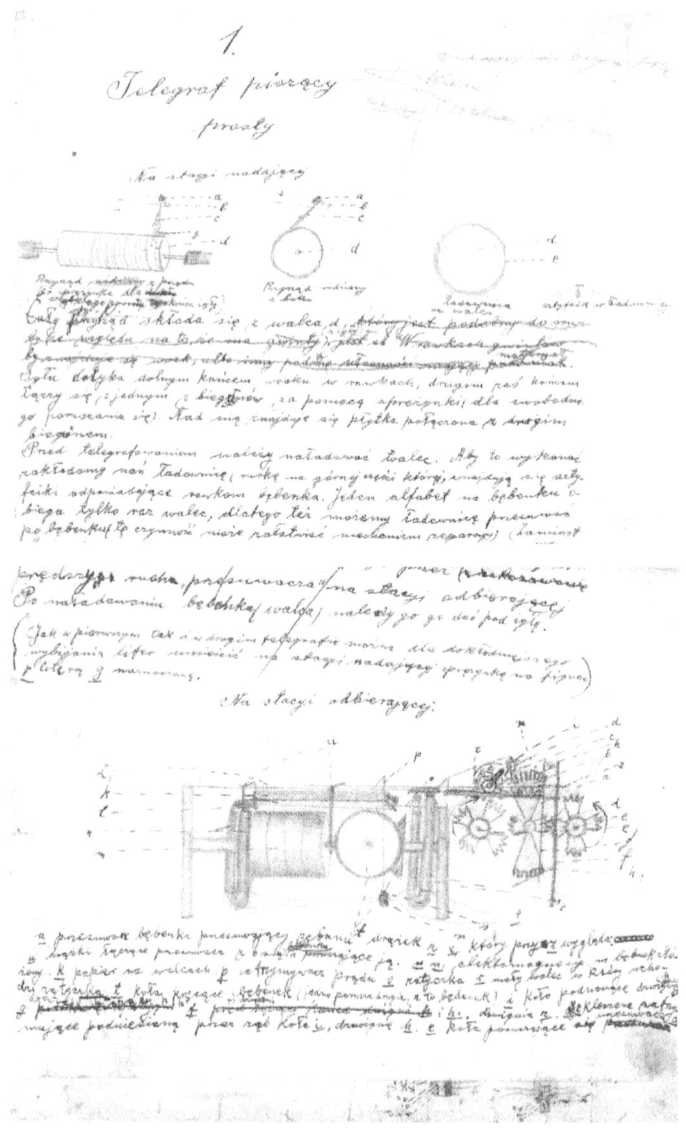
1.

Telegraf piszący

prosty

Na stacyi nadającej

Na stacyi odbierającej

Fr. Maximilian's notes and drawings about the simple writing telegraph at the broadcasting station and at the receiving station.

Na stacyi [illegible]

Telegraf złożony polega na tem, że jest złożony z więcej bębenków ra-
zem połączonych. Przy telegrafie tym nie potrzeba jak w poprzednim czę-
kać na drugą taką samą literę przez czas obiegu, gdyż, gdy np.:
telegraf jest na 4 bębenkach, to dzielimy alfabet na 4 części
i alfabety na bębenkach zaczynamy kolejno: w pierwszym od
pierwszej litery, w drugim od drugiej kolumny liter, w trzecim od trze-
ciej, a w czwartym od czwartej kolumny liter. (W ten sposób
można otrzymać w czwartej części alfabetu, cały alfabet
na wszystkich czterech bębenkach.

Na stacyi nadającej.

Na stacyi nadającej postępuje się tak jak na telegrafie poprzednim, tylko
że każdy sztyfcik ładowniczy [illegible] naraz czterech
liter, a ładownica może obracać się swobodniej. Je-
żeli chcemy umieścić literę z następnego bębenka,
[illegible] zatrzymujemy o pół miejsca następnej litery, posuwając naprzód sztyfcik o pół miejsca następnej litery, a potem posuwając go na-
wrót na swoje miejsce. Gdy chcemy wziąć liczbę z trzeciego
posuwamy sztyfcik o całą literę następną, gdy z czwartego, posuwamy o 1½ litery. Ponieważ pod czas tego zużywa się czas
musimy go także uwzględnić przy [illegible]
tem. Czas ten można także [illegible]

Second drafts concerning a compound telegraph.

Rajmund Kolbe
ucz. V-tej klasy gimnazyalnej

Description of a device that records speech and the sounds of nature.

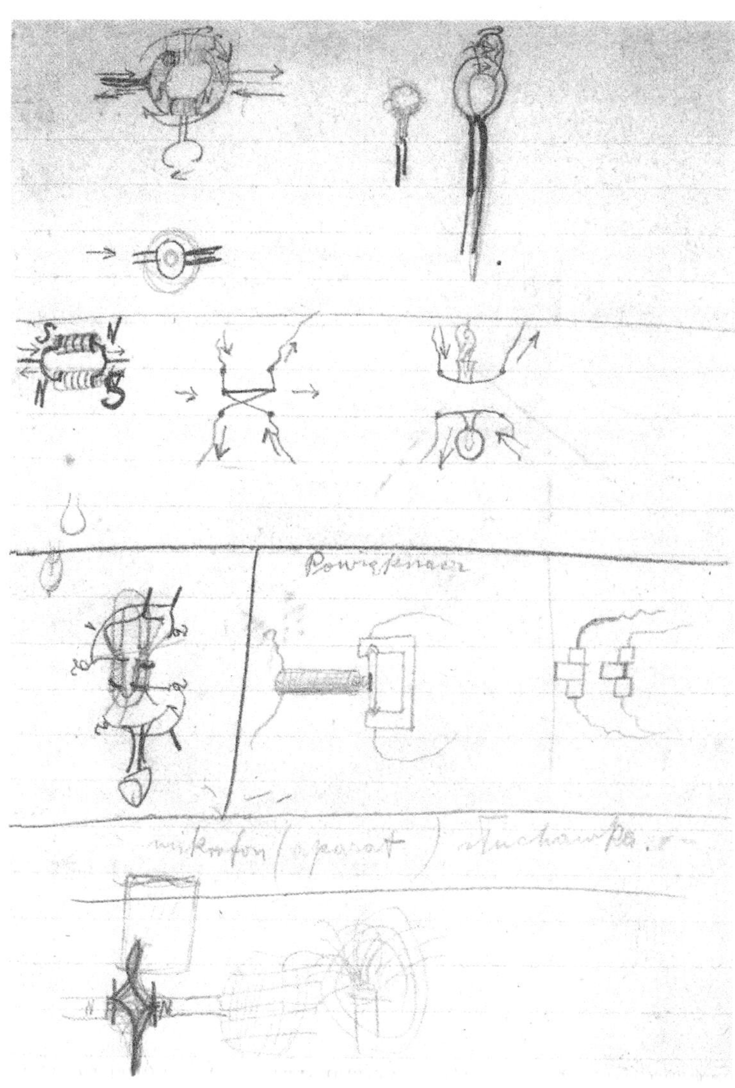

Various drawings.

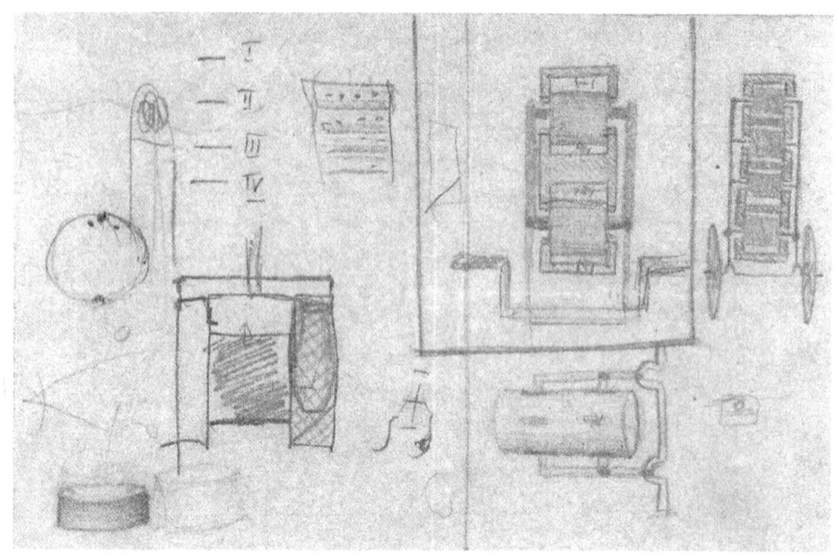

Various drawings.

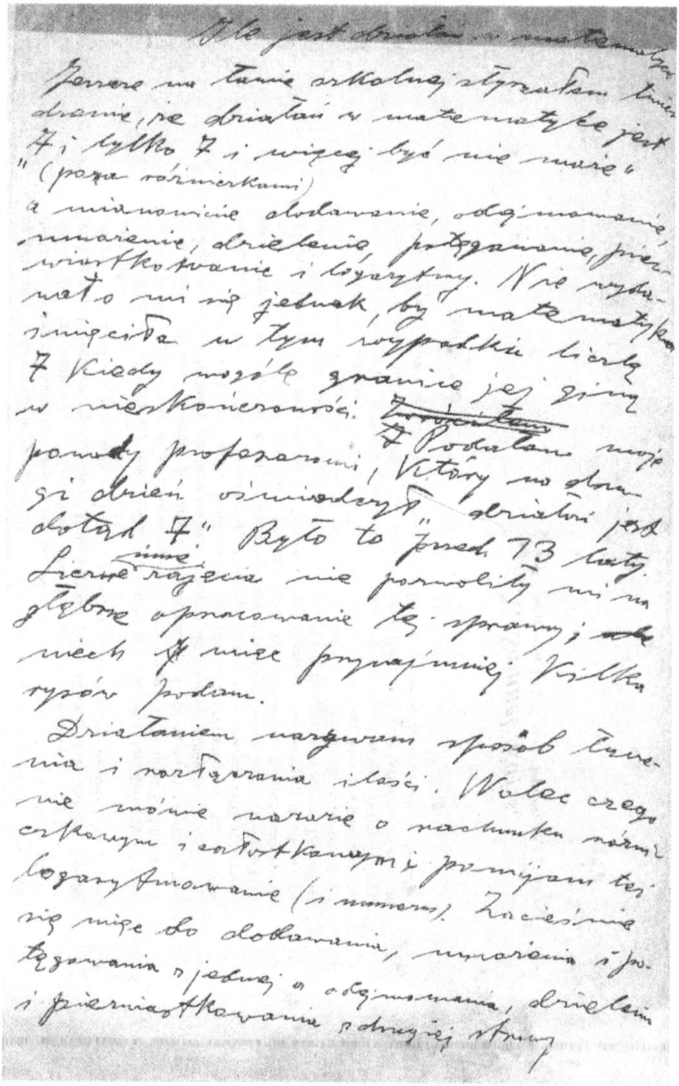
Ile jest działań w matematyce

Jeszcze na ławie szkolnej słyszałem twierdzenie, że działań w matematykę jest 7 i tylko 7 i więcej być nie może" (poza różniczkami) a mianowicie dodawanie, odejmowanie, mnożenie, dzielenie, potęgowanie, pierwiastkowanie i logarytmy. Nie wydało mi się jednak, by matematyka zamknęła w tym wypadku liczbę 7 kiedy wszystkie granice jej giną w nieskończoności. [illegible] Podałem moje powody profesorowi, który mi dnia [illegible] oświadczył "działań jest dotąd 7". Było to przed 13 laty. Liczne inne zajęcia nie pozwoliły mi na głębsze opracowanie tej sprawy, niech że choć przynajmniej kilka rysów podam.

Działaniem nazywam sposób łączenia i rozłączania ilości. Wolec czego nie mówię naraz o rachunku różniczkowym i całkowym i pomijam też logarytmowanie (i numery). Zacieśnię się więc do dodawania, mnożenia i potęgowania z jednej, a odejmowania, dzielenia i pierwiastkowania z drugiej strony

Fr. Maximilian began drafting a mathematical treatise (*KW* 1388), but other endeavors never allowed him to carry it out to completion. Mathematical formulas, written on several sheets of paper, were attached to his writing.

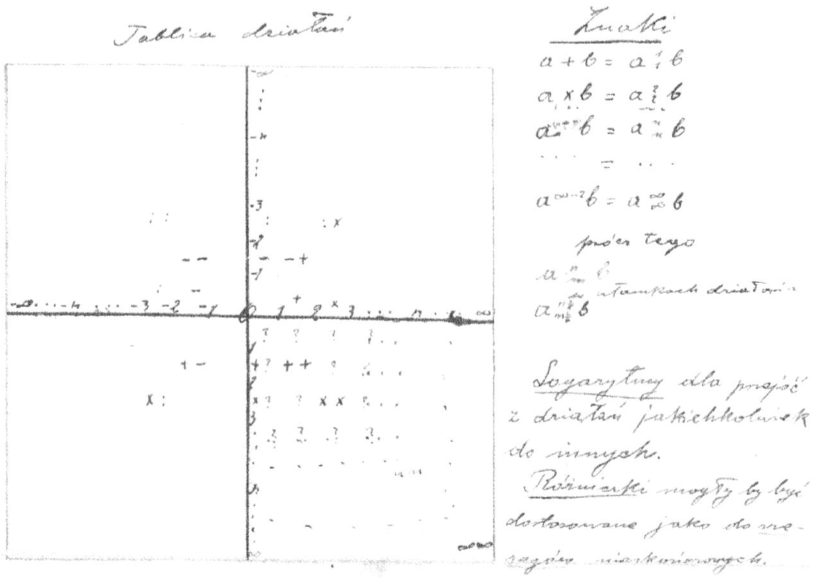
Tablica działań
Znaki
Logarytmy dla przejść z działań jakichkolwiek do innych.
Różniczki mogłyby być dostosowane jako do szeregów niezkończonych.

Sources

Foster, Claude R. *Mary's Knight: The Mission and Martyrdom of Saint Maximilian Maria Kolbe.* Rev. ed. Marytown, IL: Marytown Press, 2002.

Kalvelage, Bro. Francis M., FI. ed. *Kolbe: Saint of the Immaculata.* San Francisco: Ignatius Press, 2001.

Stone, Elaine Murray, *Maximilian Kolbe, Saint of Auschwitz.* Mahwah: Paulist Press, 1997.

Tasca, Fra. Michael. *The Writings of St. Maximilian Maria Kolbe.* 2 vols. Italy: Nervini International, 2017.

Treese, Patricia. *A Man for Others: Maximilian Kolbe.* Huntington, IN: Our Sunday Visitor, 1986. First published 1982 by Harper & Row.

Treese, Patricia. *A Man for Others: Maximilian Kolbe, "Saint of Auschwitz" In The Words of Those Who Knew Him.* Marytown, IL: Marytown Press, 1993.

Websites

About St. Maximilian Kolbe
www.marytown.com
www.mi-international.org
www.radioniepokalanow.pl (In Polish)
www.niepokalanow.eu

Amateur Radio Information

Saint Maximilian Kolbe Radio Net:
www.saintmaxnet.org

American Radio Relay League:
www.arrl.org.
www.qrz.com

Acknowledgments

When I decided to write this book, I knew that I was going outside my natural, God-given talents and would have to seek the advice and direction of a higher power, so I prayed to the Holy Spirit. I also asked St. Maximilian Kolbe and St. Francis DeSales (patron of writers) for their intercession.

However, even with the assistance of those heavenly sources, I undoubtedly, needed earthly help, people I could consult through telephone, internet and face-to-face discussions to make my book comply with journalistic standards. Furthermore, I needed cheerleaders on the sidelines encouraging me along the way to make sure I saw this to completion. So, after several years of research and writing, here are some of the names of those who were most instrumental in the final production of this book:

Sister Mary Kathleen Glavich, a Sister of Notre Dame from Chardon, Ohio, who immediately responded to me after the Catholic Writers Guild sent out an email stating that a man from North Carolina was interested in someone to copy edit a book he wrote on the life of St. Maximilian Kolbe. (Others are out there like Sister Kathleen who are willing and capable of offering their expertise and encouragement to help you overcome your self-doubt.) After reviewing her extensive resume, I knew she was the one that was to come to my rescue given her impressive career of writing more than 70 books and editing. And rescue me she did. She was great to work with, and I am very indebted to her for her patience and assistance. God bless you Sister! To find out more about her and her publications go to her website: www.kathleenglavich.org.

After receiving back the edited manuscript and making corrections, I began the process of self-publishing, still amazed that I made it into the end zone. Never give up until it's over – and it seems like it's never over!

Chris Korte, my friend and fellow author who, with his very patient and caring manner, gave absolutely essential help in getting my book printed. His experience in publishing his book, ***I Wish I Knew Then***, on Amazon's Kindle Direct Publishing, was just what I needed. I am eternally gratefully to him for working with this novice author. His book is an invaluable, practical guide offering insights for dealing with many of life's issues we all experience in our travels through our complex and often troubling world. Chris draws on his own life as well as that of experts who have had years and years of ups and downs. His book is for all ages, and I highly recommend it.

To my parents, Vince and Mary LaMay, who raised five children with love and the appropriate discipline: Thank you for your love, and for providing us with joy and happiness, a good education and, most importantly, a solid Catholic upbringing. May you both be blessed with the joy and peace of heaven.

To my beautiful daughter Bess, who has always been a source of happiness, joy and fulfillment from the moment I first saw and held her: You have been an encourager while I was engrossed in trying to be an author. Bess, I will always love you.

To my loving wife Kay who left this world too soon from the destructive effects of breast cancer: I credit you, a former journalist and engineer, for reaching down from the heavens and pushing me to write, something that was so often necessary. (I did have this innate fear that somehow her red correction marks would suddenly appear out of nowhere on my manuscript but none ever did. Sister Kathleen made up for it.) I hope that you are experiencing joy and peace in heaven and helping me follow through on my journey.

To my siblings, Jack, Jim, Tom and Kay (Kingsbury) and other relatives to numerous to mention: I thank you for the encouragement and inquiries on when the book will be finished. It helped to have that family pressure to get it done.

To the many parishioners at St. Matthew Catholic Church in Charlotte, NC, as well as a myriad of neighbors and other friends: I sincerely appreciate your support, encouragement and prayers.

To David Galusha, Ralph Sullivan, Deacon Paul Herman and fellow parishioners at St. Matthew Catholic Church, who reviewed my manuscript and gave invaluable assistance and suggestions: Thank you for your time, talents and encouragement and for keeping me on track.

To the staff at the National Shrine of St. Maximilian Kolbe, Libertyville, IL: My sincerest gratitude for your willingness to share information and material which was needed to complete this book. May your efforts continue to bring others to Christ through the martyrdom of St. Maximilian.

To the Mission of the Immaculata USA, Peoria, IL: I extend my gratitude for the many times I called and pestered the staff about where to find this or your permission to use that. You made this struggling author feel welcomed and were most helpful. May my book help to bring more members to the MI.

About the Author

William LaMay (Bill) is a native of Auburn, NY, where he attended Catholic schools through his first year in high school. In 1957, his family moved to Hyattsville, MD, where he completed his high school education in public schools. In 1966, he began his fire service career with the Prince George's County Fire Department, primarily working in the Investigations Division as a law enforcement officer, conducting fire investigations and subsequent criminal investigations of arson and bomb-related incidents.

After he retired from that job in July 1985, he and his wife moved from College Park, MD, to Charlotte, NC. There he became employed by the Mecklenburg County Fire Marshal's Office in March 1986. He retired from there in June 2006.

He is a graduate of Montgomery College, Rockville, MD, and the University of Maryland, College Park. He has taught fire science classes at several community colleges in Maryland and North Carolina.

Since retiring, he devotes much of his time practicing his faith through serving in several ministries at St. Matthew Catholic Church, Charlotte, as well as volunteering with Catholic Charities of the Diocese of Charlotte. He is an associate with the Missionaries of the Poor, Monroe, NC, and has traveled on mission trips to their missions in Kingston, Jamaica, and Cap Haitian, Haiti. He also volunteers with Hands for Haiti. A few hours each week, in honor of his late wife, he volunteers at the St. Jude Affiliate Clinic, a part of Presbyterian Hospital in Charlotte. He is also proud to be a ham radio operator.

All profits from the sale of the book will be donated to charity.

Bill can be contacted at hamoperk3rmw@gmail.com.

Printed in Great Britain
by Amazon

58443477R00089